Piec-liqué

Curves the New Way

Sharon Schamber

American Quilter's Society

P. O. Box 3290 • Paducah, KY 42002-3290
www.AmericanQuilter.com

Located in Paducah, Kentucky, the American Quilter's Society (AQS) is dedicated to promoting the accomplishments of today's quilters. Through its publications and events, AQS strives to honor today's quiltmakers and their work and to inspire future creativity and innovation in quiltmaking.

EDITOR: BARBARA SMITH
GRAPHIC DESIGN: ELAINE WILSON
ILLUSTRATIONS: SHARON SCHAMBER
COVER DESIGN: MICHAEL BUCKINGHAM
PHOTOGRAPHY: CHARLES R. LYNCH

Library of Congress Cataloging-in-Publication Data
Schamber, Sharon
 Piec-liqué : curves the new way / by Sharon Schamber.
  p.cm.
 Summary: "Author teaches machine technique for making curved piecing with speed and control. Explains four applications: layered, inset, combined and free-form. Includes three dozen block patterns"--Provided by publisher.
 ISBN 1-57432-880-8
 1. Machine quilting--Patterns. 2. Patchwork--Patterns. I. Title.

 TT835.S297 2005
 746.46--dc22

                                    2005006316

Additional copies of this book may be ordered from the American Quilter's Society, PO Box 3290, Paducah, KY 42002-3290; 800-626-5420 (orders only please); or online at www.AmericanQuilter.com. For all other inquiries, call 270-898-7903.

Dedication

This book is dedicated to my husband, Gene. I wouldn't be able to do anything without him.

To my three children, Cristy, Neil, and Quinn. They all are the joy of my life.

SEW SWEET BASKET 60" x 60". See pages 63–67 for instructions.

Acknowledgments

There are so many people I want to thank for the support they have given me in writing this book:

My husband, Gene, who makes my life easier and keeps me calm. I want to thank him for his endless support and love.

My daughter, Cristy, for her help every step of the way. She would edit when she had time and helped me when no one else could. She made sense out of the babble that sometimes comes with a creative mind.

My son Quinn, for all his help with my computer and the many new programs I had to learn. He also inspired me with his talent in painting and his ever-happy mood.

My son Neil, for laughing at me when I had too much going on. He helps me keep my balance.

My students, who kept after me to write this book.

To my oldest and dearest friend, Diana Towsley, for all the unconditional support through the years. I am glad we found each other again.

Nancy Johnson-Srebro, for her support and for pushing me in the right direction and sharing all her secrets with me.

Marget Koonz, for her dear friendship and support.

Terry White, one of the best teachers I know. Although we are new friends, we have been friends forever. I love the time we spend together, dreaming of new and exciting designs and techniques. She is my mirror spirit, and I will be her friend forever.

Russell Scott and his staff at Sewing Arts Center. They gave me wings to fly and supported anything I wanted to teach at their wonderful store. Bless you all.

Bob and Sandy Boyd at Glenwood Sewing Center.

The AQS staff. I have enjoyed working with you.

I would also like to thank the many companies that have supported me with products and supplies used in this project:

American & Efird, Inc., and Marci Brier for Mettler® and Signature® threads

Valdani Threads

Bernina® of America and Husqvarna Viking for the use of sewing machines

Prym-Dritz/Omnigrid® for notions, rotary cutters, rulers and mats

The Warm™ Company for batting

Fairfield Processing Corp. for batting

Robert Kaufman for fabric

Timeless Treasures for fabric

Star Fabrics for hand-dyed fabric

Contents

Broken Tile Block 32

Shooting Marbles Quilt 37

Spinning Dozen 45

Four Leaf Clovers 48

Spring Basket 46

Churn Churn Churn 49

Grape Basket 47

LeAnn's Pinwheel 50

Contents

Quilt Projects cont.

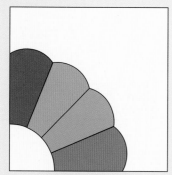

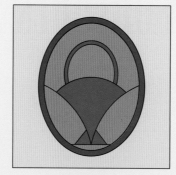

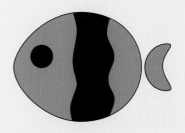

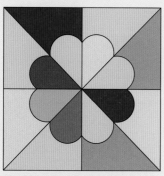

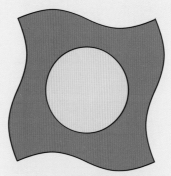

More Block Patterns 85

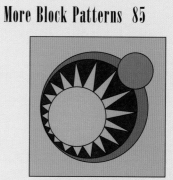

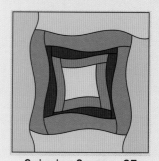

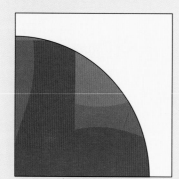

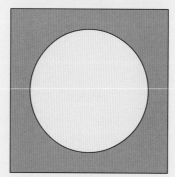

Susie Q 89

Magic Flame 94

Dove of Peace 98

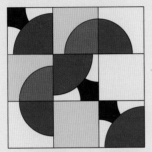

Delicate Doves 90

Blue Bells in My Garden 95

Morning Breeze 99

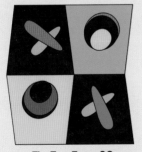

Too Many Daisies 91

Quiet Dreams 96

Crimson Iris 100

Tic Tac Toe 92

Wild Rose 97

The Discovery

I spent 20 years designing and mass-producing couture bridal gowns and formals. In that capacity, I had to develop efficient methods for constructing these complicated gowns, while maintaining quality, and making them simple to sew but intricate in their final appearance.

I also developed a technique for producing bridal headpieces. In that application, I used permanent glue instead of sewing them together. At that time, there was no water-soluble glue for basting.

The transfer of these couture techniques to quiltmaking was natural to me. I needed more control in my curved seams than the traditional method of using tick marks could give me. I also found that the time it took to mark curved pieces made piecing them a long and arduous task, and the resulting seam was not as accurate and flat as I demand in my work.

For my quilt projects, I work from the wrong side, exactly like I did in making gowns. This gives me a unique perspective on curved piecing. To me, a curved seam in a quilt is like a princess line in an expensive bridal gown. The princess seam consists of two different grain lines sewn together to create a visible seam. The seams have to match and look good at the same time or the whole gown will not work. It's the same for curved piecing in a quilt, which is actually easier … we quilter's work with one dimension, whereas a gown has three dimensions.

The need to produce quilt projects fast and accurately, and my experience in working with couture and the wonderful glue products we now have on the market, led to a discovery. As in any discovery, I stumbled onto Piec-liqué by accident.

While readying a gentle curve for appliqué, I turned the edge and glue-basted it down. Being impatient that day, I hit it with a hot iron to dry the glue faster. Then I started to appliqué the piece in place. Just by habit, I turned the project to the wrong side and flattened the seam with my iron. I was surprised to see the sharp crease that was left by the pressing. It was a short leap to knowing that the pressed crease was where I needed to sew.

I am passionate about machine work and jumped at the opportunity to machine piece the curve. I fully expected to have to take the seam out, but I couldn't resist putting the piece under the needle. The sewing went so smoothly and the glue baste was so strong that there was no shifting of the fabrics at all.

With my discovery of Piec-liqué, I have brought the techniques that I used in mass production together and have found that they are unique in the quilt world. This way of thinking is natural to me, so I want to pass the secrets on to my students.

Piec-liqué is not meant to replace appliqué. Nothing can replace the beautiful intricate details that can be achieved with appliqué. Piec-liqué was developed as a technique to use in addition to regular piecing and appliqué. For example, those seams that are gently curved can be done with Piec-liqué instead of appliqué. I recommend that you make the sample pattern that accompanies each of the four Piec-liqué techniques before making any of the patterns on pages 43–100.

OUR CHILDREN OF FREEDOM (93" x 85"). This is the first quilt I made with Piec-liqué.

Introduction to Piec-liqué

Traditional balanced

Traditional not balanced

Contemporary balanced

Contemporary not balanced

Abstract balanced

Abstract not balanced

Fig. 1. Examples of balance

Preparation

With Piec-liqué, you will no longer need to use pins to sew curved seams. There are four applications for Piec-liqué: *inset* for enclosed shapes, *layered* for gently curved seams, *split-seam* for seams interrupted by other elements, and *free-form* for spontaneous piecing without templates.

Selecting Fabrics

When choosing fabrics, always remember that the contrast and the balance of values (light, medium, and dark) are the most important qualities. I always lay the fabrics for a quilt on my cutting table and arrange them in order by contrast and value. Very shortly, it becomes apparent if there is a problem. I have found that most problems go back to the fact that there isn't enough contrast in the colors chosen. It never seems to be the colors themselves.

I have analyzed the way I think about selecting fabrics for my quilts. Basically, I divide them into one-fourth light, one-fourth dark, and one-half medium. For example, if you are using 12 fabrics, three would be dark, three would be light, and six would be medium. This is not an absolute formula, but it is a basic format to work with. Figure 1 shows examples of good contrast and balance for three basic quilt styles: traditional, contemporary, and abstract.

The balance of values can change depending on the feeling you want to achieve. Medium values make people feel comfortable. Lights and brights are exciting, and darks create a feeling of depth and interest.

For a more exciting quilt, you can add lights and take away an equal number of mediums. In the example of 12 fabrics, the proportion would then be four light, five medium, and three dark. For a more interesting quilt, add darks and take away an equal number of mediums; for example, three light, five medium, and four dark. For something that is both exciting and interesting, try a proportion of four light, four medium, and four dark. When you buy fabrics for your stash, remember to buy with those proportions in mind.

When making a quilt for decorating purposes only, replace a light and a dark with mediums. For instance, if you need 12 fabrics, select two lights, two darks, and eight mediums. These quilts have a calming effect on us, so we can live with them in our environment on a daily basis.

Gathering Supplies

You will need the following supplies for your Piec-liqué projects:

Freezer paper

Spray starch (use medium, not heavy, starch and do not substitute sizing)

Stencil brush (medium size)

Large tweezers with angled ends

Water-soluble glue (washable school glue works)

Fine tip for glue bottle (found in tole painting supplies)

Scissors (a single pair for both paper and fabric)

Basic sewing supplies

Sewing machine (in good working order)

75/11 machine embroidery needles

60-weight cotton embroidery thread (gray or beige)

Machine throat plate with single needle hole preferred

Iron (no steam, a travel iron that gets very hot is ideal)

Making Layered Templates

For Piec-liqué, use a double layer of freezer paper to make your templates. Through trial and error, I have found that preshrinking the freezer paper first eliminates many problems. Most people don't know that freezer paper shrinks in width. The amount is about ⅛" for every

Sharon's Hints

▶ If you are stumped or in a rut with color, try moving your stash or covering it up for a while, so when you see it again, you can work with fresh eyes.

▶ It is always fun to get some friends together with the challenge of using fabrics the others have chosen.

▶ I suggest using many more than 12 fabrics in your quilts. Just remember to divide them in the proportion of light, medium, and dark.

10", so if you are making a 40" piece, the paper will shrink ½" in width. This means that, if your quilt is supposed to be 40" x 40" and you don't preshrink your paper, the quilt will end up 39½" x 40".

Use the following instructions to make double-layered freezer-paper templates:

1 Cut two pieces of freezer paper (both 1" to 2" larger than the pattern).

2 Press the dull side of each piece with a hot, dry iron.

3 Spray-starch the dull side of one of the pieces. You will notice the paper rippling. Press again to flatten the paper. Repeat for the other piece.

4 Layer both pieces shiny side down and press the pieces together.

5 Trace your pattern on the dull side of the layered pieces with a permanent-ink pen. Include all numbers.

6 Add a ¾" allowance around the outside of the block pattern (see Notes). Your double-layered freezer paper pattern is ready to cut into individual templates.

7 Make another copy of the whole design, with numbers, to use as a placement guide. This copy can be on freezer paper or parchment paper.

NOTES

▶ Unfinished blocks are approximately 1½" larger than the finished size to allow for distortion during sewing. The excess fabric will be trimmed off when you true up the sewn block.

▶ Because the Piec-liqué templates will be placed on the wrong sides of the fabrics, the patterns for asymmetrical designs are mirror images of the blocks pictured.

▶ For your convenience, each pattern is accompanied by a Block Resizing chart that you can use to enlarge blocks for other projects. For the quilt projects, use the patterns at the size given unless instructed otherwise.

Creating a Pressing Surface

In my time teaching, I have found that most problems come from the pressing surface used. It is important to use a surface that is hard and flat. It also needs to have a small amount of grip. Therefore, I am including instructions for making a pressing board (fig. 2). My students have found that this board not only helps with Piec-liqué but also with regular piecing. The board can be modified to suit your personal needs.

1 Cut a piece of chipboard that is 14" x 19" and round off the corners.

2 Spray a small amount of adhesive on the board and place a piece of 100 percent cotton batting, 13½" x 18½", on top of the sprayed board.

3 Fuse a piece of fusible web, 13" x 18", to the batting. Then pull the paper off the web.

4 Center a canvas piece, 19" x 24", on the board. Use a hot iron to press it firmly to the batting. The fusible web will secure all the layers together.

5 Using a staple gun, staple the canvas to the back of the chipboard. Finish the back with a piece of felt, or you can glue a cutting mat to the back.

Setting Up Your Sewing Machine

Set your machine up with a size 75 embroidery needle, 60-weight cotton embroidery thread, 12 stitches per inch, and a single-needle throat plate, if possible.

Use a ¼" foot, if you have one. As you sew, you will need to be able to see the seam allowance fold line just as it gets to the needle. This narrow foot will allow you to do this.

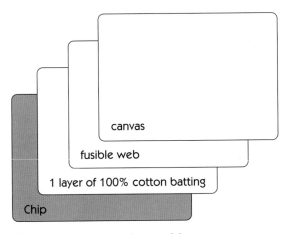

Fig. 2. Pressing board assembly

NOTE

▶ **Sew important...** for all of the techniques, if you come to an area of the seam that is cupping and not lying flat, put a few small clips in the allowance to relax the seam.

Sharon's Hints

▶ To cut multiple templates at the same time, you can stack the layered freezer-paper sheets up to four deep and staple the pattern on top of the stack. Be sure to use a good pair of scissors to cut through all the layers. The template's edges need to be smooth, because whatever kinks you leave on the edges will show up in your finished project.

▶ The freezer-paper templates can be reused several times. I have used templates up to 10 times.

▶ Pattern pieces that lie on the outside edge of the block need to have a ¾" allowance on the outside edges and a ⅜" allowance on the inside edges.

▶ It's easier to keep track if you do not cut all the template pieces at once.

▶ If you cannot see the fold line, I have found that it helps to mark it with a washout marking pen.

▶ I like to use tweezers when I sew. They help to flatten the seam, and they work as small fingers holding the seam allowances in place.

Inset

The inset technique includes the circle or any enclosed shape with gentle curves.

Marble Block

Making the Marble Block

1. Use the Marble block pattern (page 17) to prepare a double-layered template as described on pages 11 and 12.

2. Cut the template square on the line then carefully cut out the circle. You can discard the circle. The square piece is your template.

3. Cut a 7½" fabric square for the block background. Center the template, shiny side down, on the wrong side of the fabric square and, using a hot, dry iron, press to adhere the template to the fabric (fig. 1).

Fig. 1

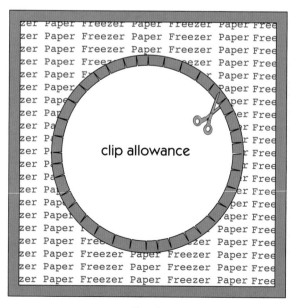

Fig. 2

4. Cut out the fabric circle, leaving a ⅜" turn-under allowance all around, by eye. Clip the allowance every ¼" (fig. 2).

5. Spray some starch in the spray can lid. Working with only a quarter of the circle at a time, saturate your stencil brush with starch and paint the allowance.

6. With the iron in one hand, use your free hand to fold the allowance over the edge of the template and press as you go. Press dry. Repeat for the other quarter sections of the circle (fig. 3).

7. Let the piece cool slightly. Pull the template off the fabric. Turn the piece wrong side up, lightly press it with your iron to set the fold, and restore the original shape.

8. With the piece wrong side up, place a fine line of water-soluble glue (shown in red) around the very edge of the circle (fig. 4).

Sharon's Hints

▸ When you are sewing, the extra fabric will give you something to hold onto, allowing control of even the smallest circle. Because the seams are secured with starch and glue, they will sew smoothly and evenly.

▸ If you cannot see the fold line, it helps to mark it with a washout marking pen.

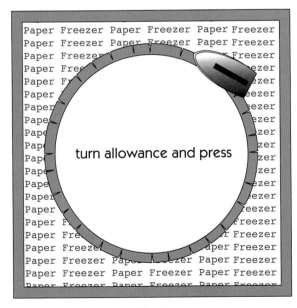

Fig. 3

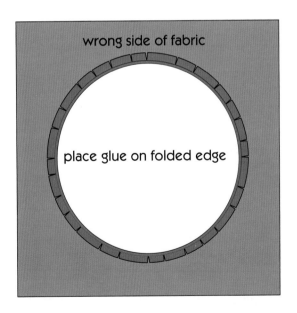

Fig. 4

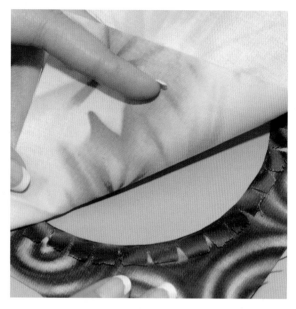

Fig. 5

9. For the inset circle piece, cut a fabric square 7½". Before the glue dries, place the square, wrong side up, on top of the prepared piece. Press to dry the glue, which will heat-set the two pieces together (fig. 5).

10. Turn the block right side up. Lift the top piece to expose the fold. Keep lifting the top piece out of the way as you sew around the circle in the fold (fig. 6). Trim the excess circle fabric even with the edge of the allowance (fig. 7). Press. Making sure that the circle is centered in the block, trim it to 6½".

Fig. 6

Fig. 7

Sharon's Hints

▶ If you want the allowances to go toward the center of the circle, just wet the seam with water and press. This makes the piece look more like appliqué.

Marble Block Pattern

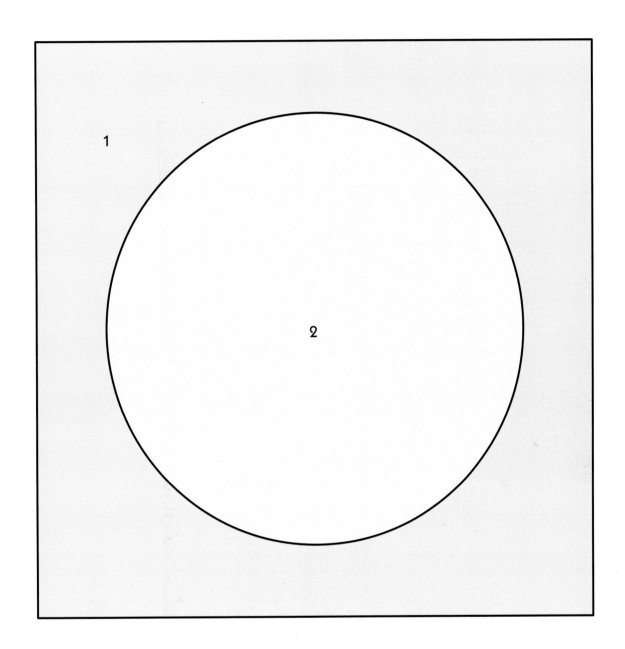

Block Resizing

6"	100%
8"	134%
10"	167%
12"	200%
14"	234%

Piece numbers = layering order

You need extra-wide seam allowances for Piec-liqué:

    After enlarging (if desired), add a ¾" allowance around outside of the block pattern.

    Add ⅜" allowances to inside seams, by eye, as you cut fabric pieces.

After sewing, square and trim the block, leaving a ¼" seam allowance all around.

The layered technique is for gently curved seams. Notice that the sample block is asymmetrical, so the pattern is a mirror image of the finished block. Because templates will be placed on the wrong sides of the fabrics, the finished block will end up oriented properly.

Star Fish Block

Making the Starfish Block

1. If desired, you can enlarge the Starfish block pattern on page 22. Then add a ¾" seam allowance around the outside of the block.

*Place all pieces **wrong side up** on the placement guide.*

2. Prepare a double-layered template and a placement guide as described on page 11. Press template 1, shiny side down, on the wrong side of your chosen fabric. Cut out the fabric shape, adding a ⅜" allowance by eye as you cut. Clip only the inside curves every ¼" (fig. 1).

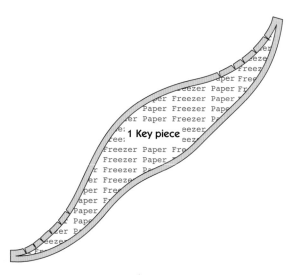

Fig. 1

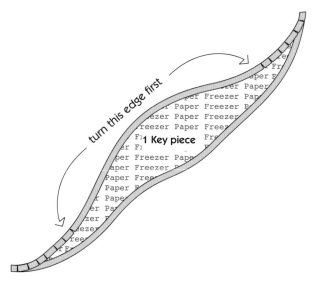

Fig. 2

3. Spray some starch in the spray can lid. Saturate the stencil brush with starch and paint the allowance along the top edge. Use your iron to turn that edge to the back (fig. 2). Press dry. Leave the template in place and wait to turn the other edge until step 8.

4. Place piece 1 on the placement guide (fig. 3). Pin in place. Repeat the preparation process with piece 2, turning the allowance where shown in figure 4. Remove the freezer paper and use your iron to lightly set the fold and press the piece back into shape (fig. 5).

Key Piece

Some of the patterns have key pieces. All the edges of key pieces are turned to the back. Key pieces are laid on the placement guide first, and they determine which edges of the remaining pieces will be turned and which will be glued; that is, if an edge will lie on an already turned edge, use glue. If an edge will lie on the placement guide, turn the edge.

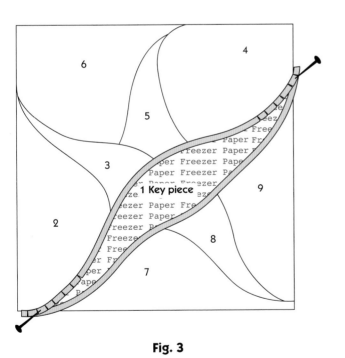

Fig. 3

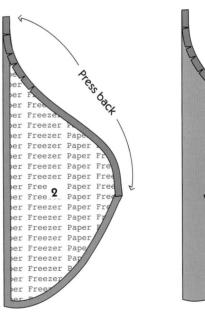

Fig. 4

Fig. 5

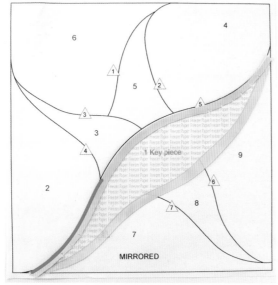

Fig. 6

5. Place a thin line of glue on the very edge of piece 1 where it will be covered by piece 2, shown in red on figure 6. Position piece 2 on the layout guide and, before the glue dries, press dry to heat-set (fig. 7).

6. For piece 3, turn the edge that will lie on the placement guide. Put a thin line of glue on the edges of pieces 1 and 2 that will be covered by the unturned edges of piece 3 (fig. 8). Place piece 3 on the guide and heat-set.

7. Prepare pieces 4 and 5, turning the appropriate edges as before and placing glue on the already turned edges of previous pieces. Place each piece on the guide in turn and heat-set. Add and heat-set piece 6, which will not need turning, only glue.

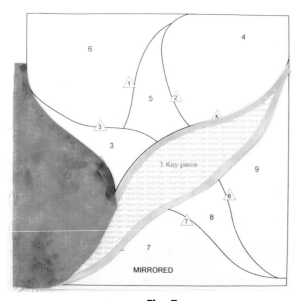

Fig. 7

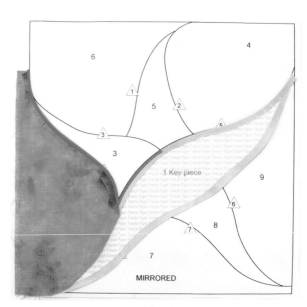

Fig. 8

8. Take the prepared section of the block off the placement guide and turn the remaining edge of piece 1. Remove the freezer paper. Put this section back on the guide (fig. 9). Secure with pins.

9. Following the same procedure you used for pieces 2–6, place pieces 7–9 on the guide. Piece 9 will not need turning, only glue (fig 10).

10. To sew, unpin the block from the placement guide and turn the block right side up. Expose the fold for seam 1. Sew along the fold. Expose seam 2 and sew along the fold. Continue sewing the rest of the seams in the same manner to complete the block.

11. Press the block and trim it, leaving a ¼" seam allowance all around the outside.

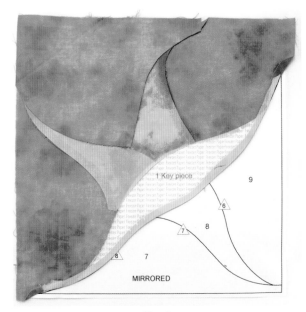

Fig. 9

Fig. 10

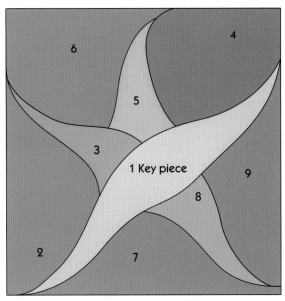

pattern on page 22

Starfish Block Pattern

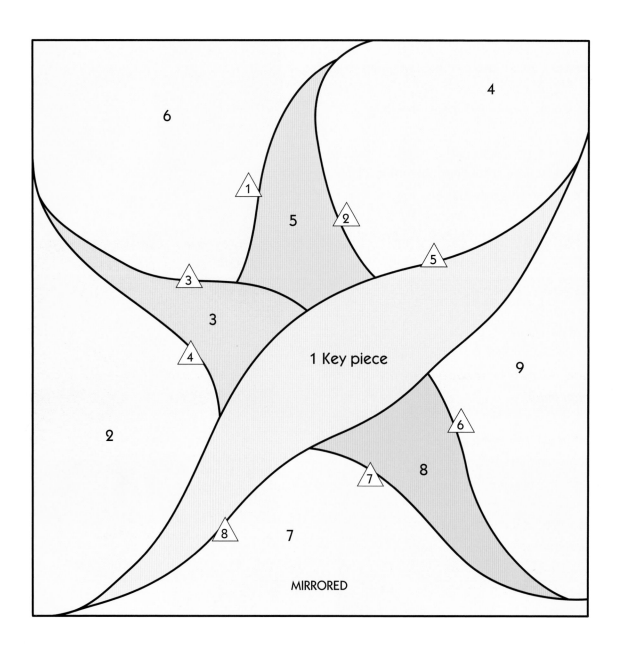

Block Resizing

6"	100%
8"	134%
10"	167%
12"	200%
14"	234%

Piece numbers = layering order
Numbers in triangles = sewing sequence for seams
You need extra-wide seam allowances for Piec-liqué:
    After enlarging (if desired), add a ¾" allowance around outside of the block pattern.
    Add ⅜" allowances to inside seams, by eye, as you cut fabric pieces.
After sewing, square and trim the block, leaving a ¼" seam allowance all around.

Split-Seam

The split-seam (or combined) technique differs from the layered technique in that a seam or several seams are interrupted by other elements. A split seam in the Moon River block occurs along the bottom edge of piece 1 (see pattern on page 26).

Making the Moon River Block

1. If desired, you can enlarge the Moon River block pattern (pattern and Block Resizing, page 26). Then add a ¾" seam allowance around the outside of the block.

*Place all pieces **wrong side up** on the placement guide.*

2. Prepare a double-layered template and a placement guide as described on page 11. Press template 1, shiny side down, on the wrong side of your chosen fabric. Cut the fabric shape, adding a ⅜" turn-under allowance by eye as you cut. Clip the inside curve every ¼".

3. Spray some starch in the spray can lid. Working with a section at a time, saturate your stencil brush with starch and paint the allowance. Use a hot, dry iron to fold the allowances to the back. Press dry. Do not turn the ends of piece 1. They will be hidden by pieces 2 and 4.

Moon River Block

Note

Notice that the block is asymmetrical, so that the pattern is a mirror image of the finished block. Because templates are placed on the wrong side of the fabrics, the finished block will end up in the same orientation as the block in the picture.

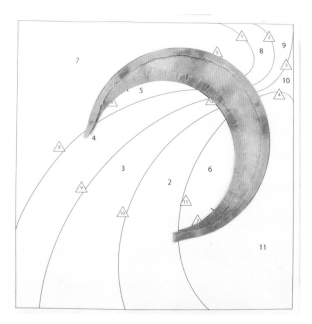

Fig. 1

4. Remove the freezer paper. Place piece 1 on the placement guide and pin (fig. 1). In the same way, prepare piece 2, turning both curved edges. Leave the ends unturned. Place piece 2 on the guide (fig. 2). Pin in place.

5. Prepare piece 3, but turn only the edge that lies next to piece 4. Place a thin line of glue on the very edge of piece 2 where it will be covered by piece 3. Place piece 3 on the guide and, before the glue dries, press to heat-set.

6. Prepare piece 4, turning only the edge that lies next to piece 7. Place a thin line of glue on the edge of piece 3. Place piece 4 on the guide and heat-set. Make sure that the ends of piece 1 lie on top of pieces 2 and 4 (fig. 3).

Resist the temptation to take the block off the placement guide. Chances are that, if you do take it off, you will not get it back in the right position.

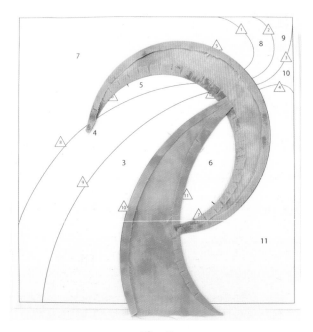

Fig. 2

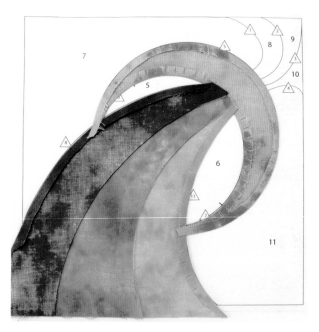

Fig. 3

7. Prepare and add the remaining pieces in the same manner, turning or gluing the appropriate edges. Pieces 5, 6, and 11 need only glue. Turn only the edge of piece 7 that borders piece 8 (fig. 4). Heat-set after each addition.

8. After all the pieces have been placed, take the block off the placement guide. Make sure that the seams are securely glued. Reglue any that seem loose.

9. To sew, turn the block right side up. Expose the fold for seam 1. Sew along the fold. Expose seam 2 and sew along the fold. Continue sewing seams 3 through 5 in the same manner.

10. Refer to the pattern. When you get to pieces 6 and 7, you will need to sew just partway (fig. 5). The places to stop sewing are marked on the pattern by short red lines crossing the seam. Finish sewing seams 8–11 (fig. 6). The final seam will be 12, connecting seams 6 and 7.

11. Press the block and trim it, leaving a ¼" seam allowance all around the outside of the block.

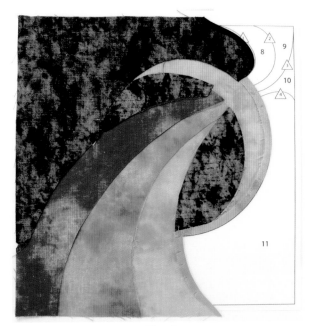

Fig. 4

Fig. 5

Fig. 6

Moon River Block Pattern

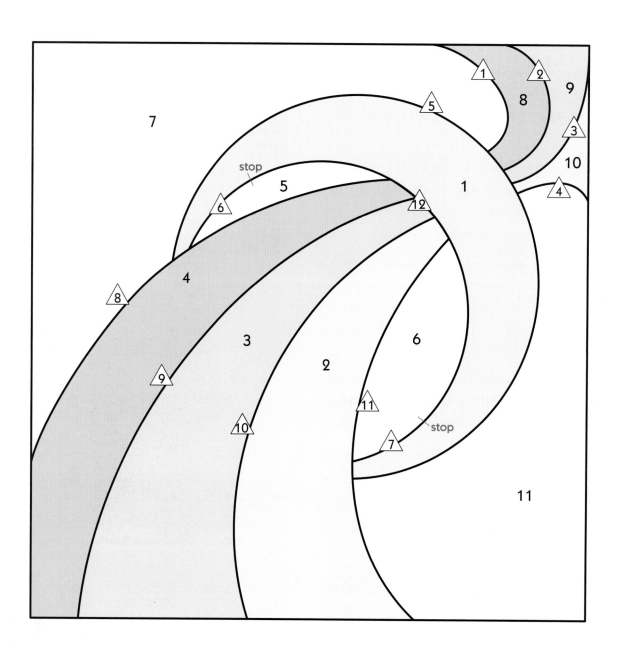

Block Resizing

6"	100%
8"	134%
10"	167%
12"	200%
14"	234%

Piece numbers = layering order

Numbers in triangles = sewing sequence for seams

You need extra-wide seam allowances for Piec-liqué:

   After enlarging (if desired), add a ¾" allowance around outside of the block pattern.

   Add ⅜" allowances to inside seams, by eye, as you cut fabric pieces.

After sewing, square and trim the block, leaving a ¼" seam allowance all around.

Free-Form

This is the most exciting form of Piec-liqué. It takes on a life of its own, but that is what makes it so wonderful. I have found that it can be used in so many ways: Hawaiian quilts, cutwork, vine and leaf borders, and landscape quilts, to name just a few.

Making a Free-Form Basket

To learn the technique, a simple basket makes a good practice piece. Then you can move on to more complicated designs.

1. If desired, you can enlarge the sample free-flow basket block pattern (pattern and Block Resizing, page 31). Then add a ¾" seam allowance around the outside of the block.

In the Free-Form method, freezer-paper templates are not used.

2. Make a placement guide from the pattern. Feel free to cut fabric pieces spontaneously and use the guide for approximate placement only.

3. For a 12" block, cut three 8" x 13½" background rectangles and one 14" square for the basket and handle.

4. Cut the 14" basket square in half diagonally. From one triangle, cut a bias strip 1" x 15" for the handle. Using your stencil brush, put a small amount of starch along one long side of the handle strip. Press that edge to the center of the strip, right side out. Repeat for the other side of the strip. The two edges should touch in the center (fig. 1).

Free-Form Basket

Fig. 1

Fig. 2

Unlike the other Piec-liqué techniques, place all free-form pieces right side up on the placement guide.

5. Place the handle on your placement guide. Very gently press the handle into shape (fig. 2). You may need to use more starch to get it to hold its shape. Remove the handle from the guide.

6. Align a background rectangle on the guide. Leave ¾" of background beyond the guide on both sides and at the top. (If you cannot see the guide through the fabric, use a light source.) Pin the handle in position.

7. Lift up half the handle and place a fine line of glue on both folded edges. Reposition and heat-set. Repeat for the other half.

8. Turn the piece to the back and split the background down the center of the handle (fig. 3). Open the split to see the fold lines to sew on. Stitch in the folds then press the handle. Return the handle section to the guide.

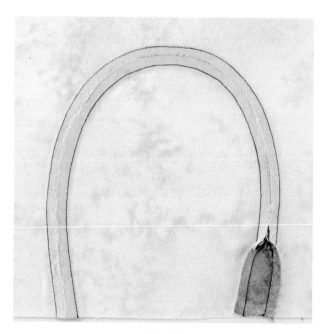

Fig. 3

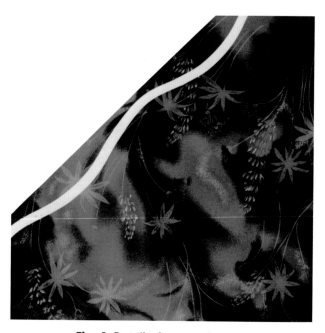

Fig. 4. Detail of serpentine cut

9. With your rotary cutter, cut a soft serpentine shape on the longest edge of the remaining basket triangle (fig. 4). Put a few small clips, about ¼" apart, in the inside curves.

10. Starch and turn the serpentine edge (fig. 5). The fold doesn't need to be exact, but it needs to be smooth. If the edge becomes distorted, lightly block it into shape.

11. Place the prepared basket in a pleasing position on the handle section (fig. 6). Secure with pins. Lift up one side of the basket and place a fine line of glue along the turned edge. Lay the basket back down and heat-set. Repeat on the other side of the basket.

12. Turn to the back of the piece and trim off excess background fabric from underneath the basket, leaving a ¼" seam allowance. Sew on the fold line and press. If the seam allowance cups on the inside curves, you can relax it with a few clips.

13. Serpentine cut the right side of the basket (fig. 7). Starch and turn the serpentine edge.

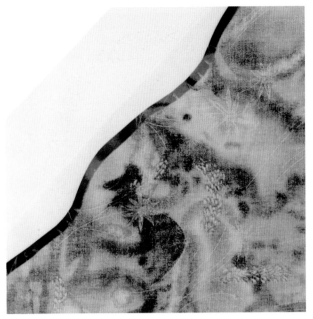

Fig. 5. Detail of turned edge

Fig. 6

Fig. 7

Fig. 8

14. For the basket base, cut a 5½" square from the triangle left over from cutting the handle. Serpentine cut the square in half diagonally. Prepare the triangles by starching and turning their serpentine edges (fig. 8).

15. Glue a prepared triangle to each of the two remaining 8" x 13½" background rectangles. Be sure to make a left and a right base/background section. (See right base/background section in figure 9). Trim, sew in the fold, and press.

16. Using the guide for alignment, glue and press the basket to the right base/background section. Trim, sew, and press.

17. Serpentine cut the left side of the basket. Starch and turn the serpentine edge (fig. 10).

18. Using the guide for alignment, glue and press the basket to the left base/background section. Trim, sew in the fold, and press. Trim the block to a 12½" square.

Fig. 9

Fig. 10

Free-Form Basket Pattern

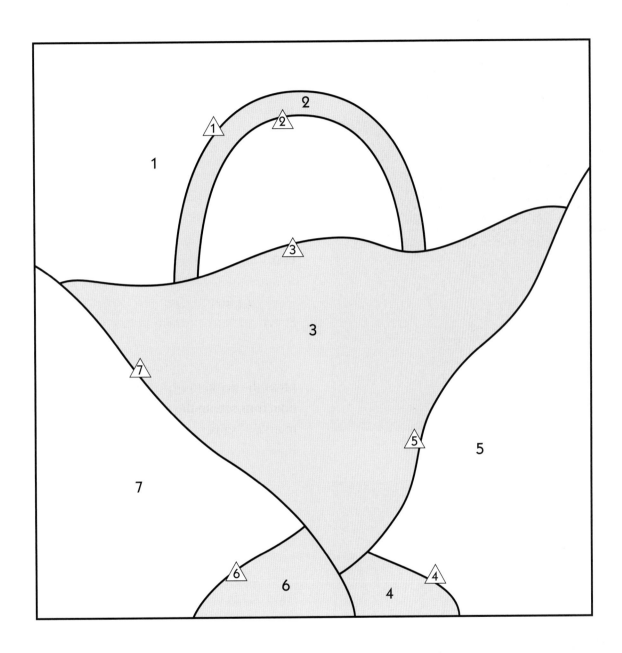

Block Resizing

6"	100%
8"	134%
10"	167%
12"	200%
14"	234%

Piece numbers = layering order

Numbers in triangles = sewing sequence for seams

You need extra-wide seam allowances for Piec-liqué:

    After enlarging (if desired), add a ¾" allowance around outside of the block pattern.

    Add ⅜" allowances to inside seams, by eye, as you cut fabric pieces.

After sewing, square and trim the block, leaving a ¼" seam allowance all around.

Starter Project

Broken Tile Block

Broken Tile Block

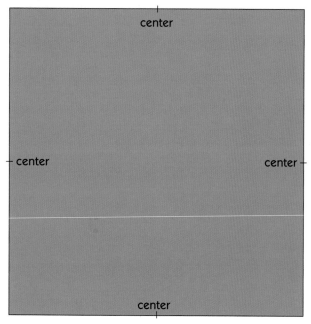

Fig. 1

Technique: layered Piec-liqué, page 18

You will be using the layered technique to make nine Broken Tile blocks. These can be used to make the SHOOTING MARBLES or the TILE FLOOR projects (pages 37 and 60).

Making the Broken Tile Block

1. For 6" finished blocks, cut an 8" square from each of nine different fabrics. (The author used nine purple fabrics in her SHOOTING MARBLES quilt).

2. Using the Broken Tile patterns on page 36, prepare nine double-layered templates of both patterns. Include the center marks on your templates.

3. Mark the centers of all four edges of each fabric square with a small clip (fig. 1).

4. Press a template 1 to the wrong side of each fabric square, matching the center marks (fig. 2).

5. Adding a ⅜" seam allowance, by eye, on both sides of the template, cut the fabric pieces (fig. 3). Clip the inside curves on the center pieces. Save the outside pieces for later.

6. Saturate your stencil brush with spray starch and paint the allowance on one side of a center piece. Use your iron to turn the allowance to the back and press it dry to heat-set. Repeat for the other side of the center piece.

7. Let the piece cool slightly then pull the freezer paper off. The fabric will be slightly distorted so press it to restore the original shape. Prepare all the center pieces in the same manner.

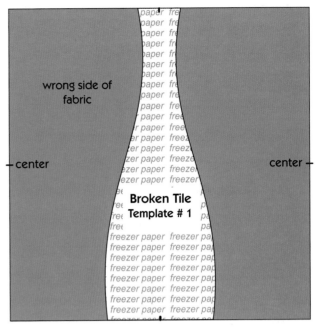

Fig. 2

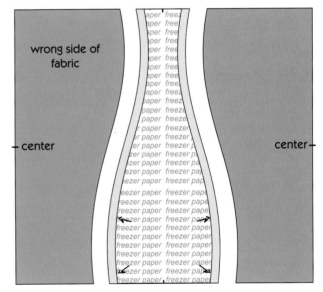

Fig. 3

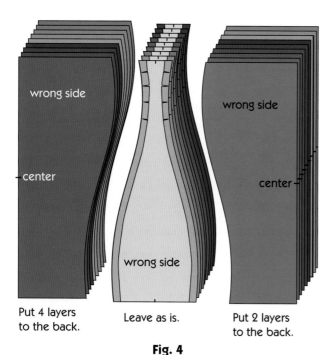

wrong side

center

wrong side

wrong side

center

Put 4 layers
to the back.

Leave as is.

Put 2 layers
to the back.

Fig. 4

8. Stack the center pieces and outside pieces, wrong side up, in order by color. For the right stack, move the top two pieces to the bottom of the stack. For the left stack, move the top four pieces to the bottom. Leave the center stack as is (fig. 4).

9. Use the top piece in each stack for the first block. Put a fine line of water-soluble glue on the very edge of both sides of the center piece. Place the outside pieces over the center piece, covering the seam allowances (fig. 5). Before the glue dries, heat-set the unit with your iron. Check to make sure that the pieces are secure.

10. To sew, turn the center piece wrong side up and lay it so you can see the fold line for one of the seams. Sew along the fold. Repeat for the other seam (fig. 6). Press all seam allowances toward the center. Repeat for all nine blocks.

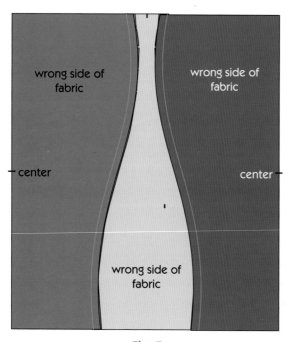

wrong side of
fabric

wrong side of
fabric

center

center

wrong side of
fabric

Fig. 5

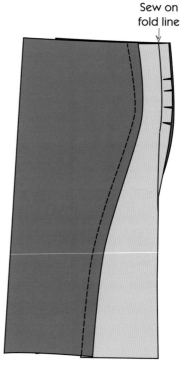

Sew on
fold line

Fig. 6

11. Turn five of the blocks with the small end of the center piece pointed to the left and the remaining blocks pointed to the right. Matching the center marks on the blocks and templates, press a template 2 to the wrong side of each block. (figs. 7a and b). Then repeat steps 4 through 7.

12. Take the two outside rows from the blocks pointing left and pair them with the center pieces of those pointing right. Take the outside rows from the blocks pointing right and pair them with the left center pieces. Feel free to play with color placement.

13. Turn the allowances under and sew the blocks as you did before. Square and trim the blocks to 6½" x 6½". If you are trimming larger blocks, see the trim sizes in the Block Resizing chart on page 36.

Sharon's Hints

▶ When you use batiks, the freezer paper adheres much more securely, making it a bit more difficult to remove. Just warm the piece with your iron, and the template will easily peel off.

▶ There may be a slight shadow of glue showing through the fabric. Because you are using water-soluble glue, it will completely dissolve with the first washing of the quilt.

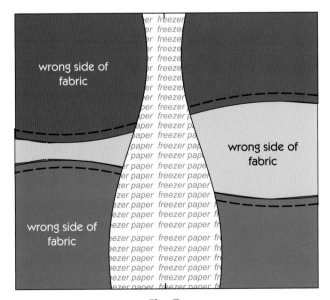

Fig. 7a

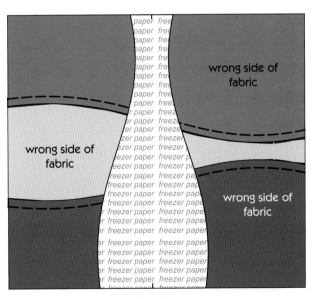

Fig. 7b

Broken Tile Patterns

Block Resizing

The pattern provided makes a 6" finished block. Use the table below to enlarge the pattern to the size desired for your project. The 12" size is recommended for ease of construction.

Size	Enlarge	Fabric Squares	Trim Size
8"	134%	10¾"	8½"
10"	167%	13⅜"	10½"
12"	200%	16"	12½"
14"	234%	18¾"	14½"

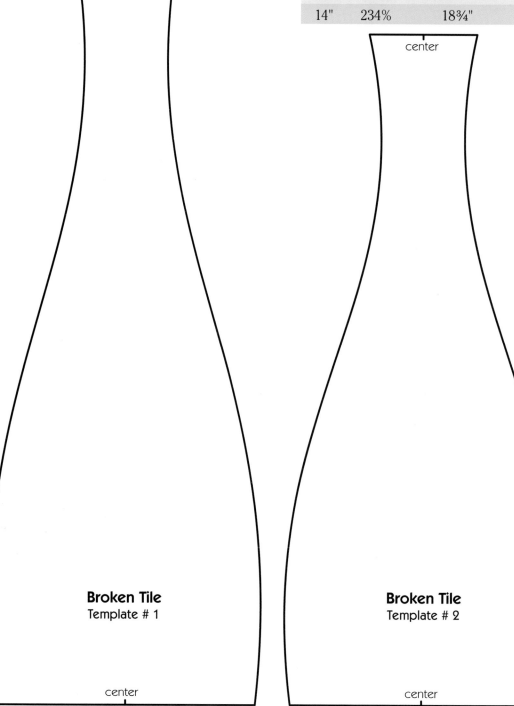

center

Broken Tile
Template # 1

center

center

Broken Tile
Template # 2

center

Shooting Marbles Quilt

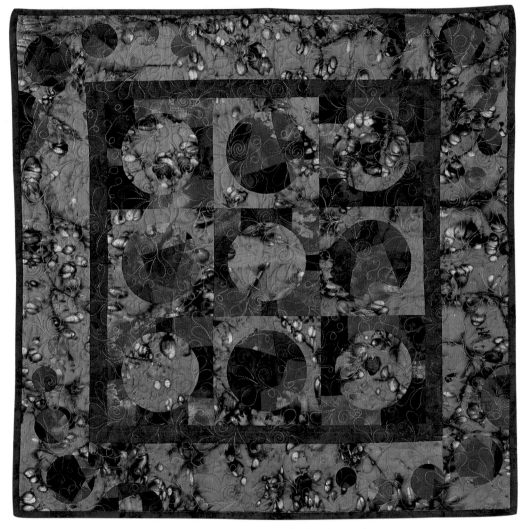

SHOOTING MARBLES, 28" x 28", by the author

Quilt size: 28" x 28" before quilting
Block size: 6" finished

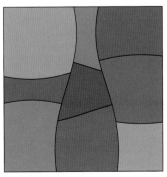

Broken Tile Block 32

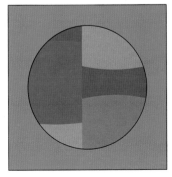

Marble Block 14

Fig. 1

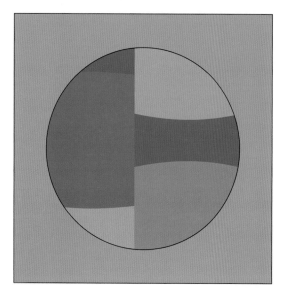

Fig. 2

Techniques: inset Piec-liqué, page 14
layered Piec-liqué, page 18

You will be using the layered technique to make the Broken Tile blocks and the inset technique to turn the Broken Tile blocks into Marble blocks.

Making a 28" Quilt

Cutting Guide

A	pattern A
B	pattern A, reverse colors
C	1½" x 18½"
D	1½" x 20½"
E	4½" x 20½"
F	4½" x 28½"

Making Blocks

1. Follow the instructions beginning on page 32 to make nine Broken Tile blocks (fig. 1). If you prefer, you can use nine 7½" plain fabric squares for your circles.

2. Make four Marble blocks with green on the outside and a Broken Tile block on the inside. Make five Marble blocks with the green on the inside and a Broken Tile block on the outside (fig. 2). Make sure to press the blocks flat.

3. Referring to the quilt assembly diagram (fig. 3), arrange blocks in checkerboard fashion. Press the seam allowances toward the green blocks. Sew the blocks together in rows then sew the rows together.

4. Add 1½" wide inner borders to the quilt and 4½" wide outer borders.

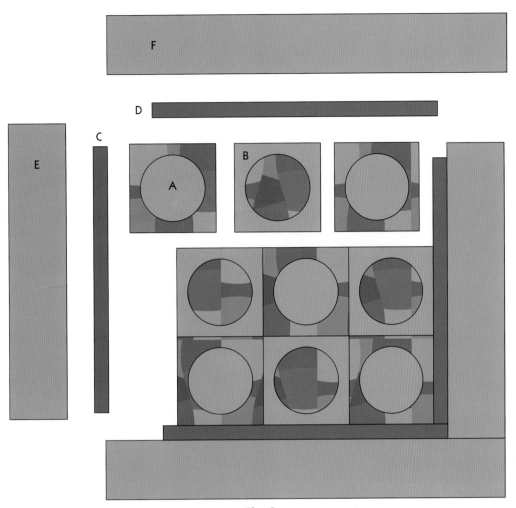

Fig. 3

ADDING MARBLES TO BORDER

1. Referring to the Block Resizing chart, enlarge the Border Marble pattern on page 41 to the same size as your blocks.

2. Prepare a layered freezer-paper template for each marble size and a marble placement guide (fig. 4). You can reuse the marble templates.

3. With the placement guide dull side up, align a corner of the quilt border, wrong side up, on the guide. Mark the placement of the marbles. Repeat for all four corners.

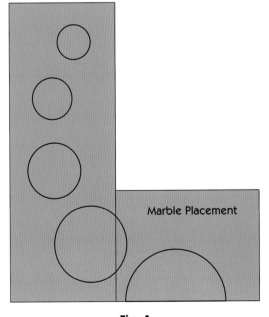

Marble Placement

Fig. 4

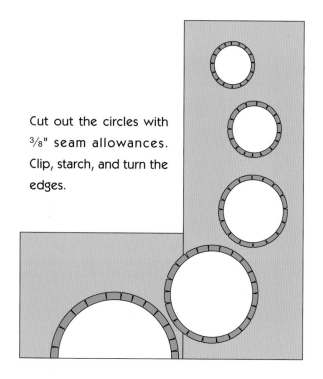

Cut out the circles with ³⁄₈" seam allowances. Clip, starch, and turn the edges.

4. Prepare Broken Tile scrap squares to fill in the marbles. (Squares need to be 3" larger than the openings.) If you run out of the scraps, you can use plain fabrics or make a few more Broken Tile blocks.

5. Referring to the Inset Technique on page 14 and figure 5, glue, sew, and trim the marble circles on all four borders.

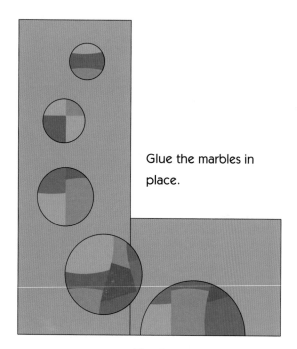

Glue the marbles in place.

Fig. 5

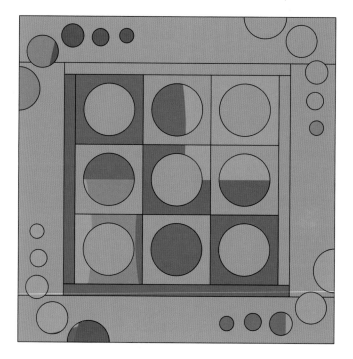

Shooting Marbles Block Pattern A

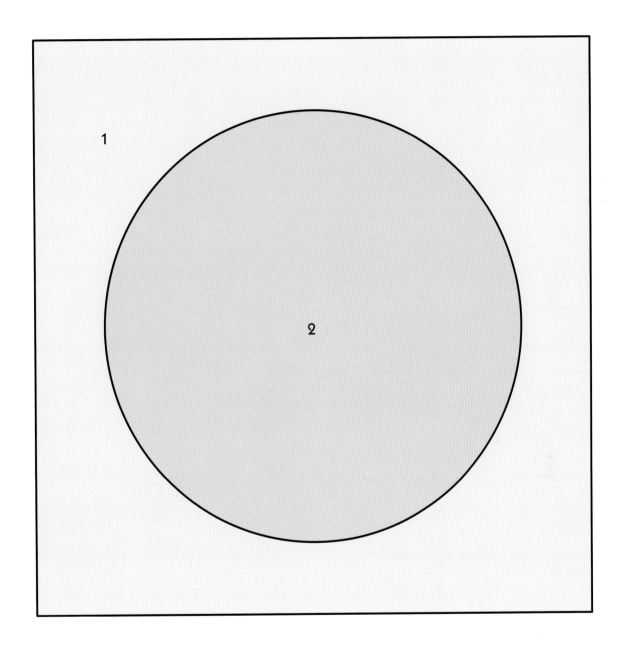

Block Resizing

Size	Percent
6"	100%
8"	134%
10"	167%
12"	200%
14"	234%

Piece numbers = layering order
You need extra-wide seam allowances for Piec-liqué:
    After enlarging (if desired), add a ¾" allowance around outside of the block pattern.
    Add ⅜" allowances to inside seams, by eye, as you cut fabric pieces.
After sewing, square and trim the block, leaving a ¼" seam allowance all around.

Marble Border Pattern

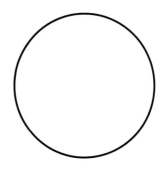

Border Resizing

6"	100%
8"	134%
10"	167%
12"	200%
14"	234%

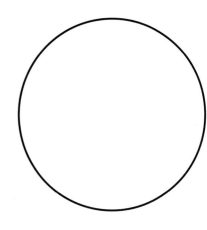

WRONG SIDE UP
Line up quilt seams
with dashed lines.

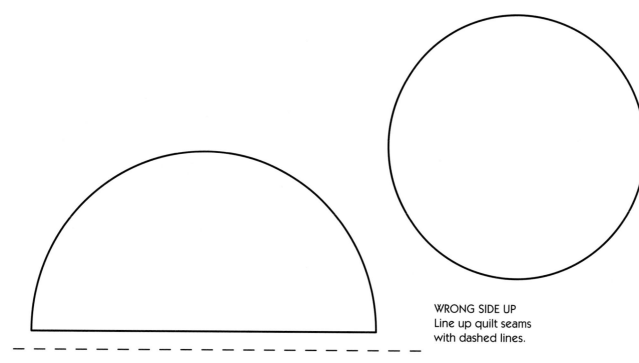

WRONG SIDE UP
Line up quilt seams
with dashed lines.

Quilt Projects

Drunkard's Path Unit

Use the Drunkard's Path pattern, at the size provided on page 44, as a unit to make the following six blocks and accompanying quilt patterns.

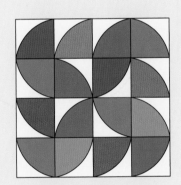

Spinning Dozen 45

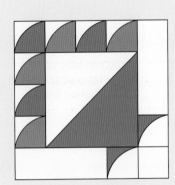

Spring Basket 46

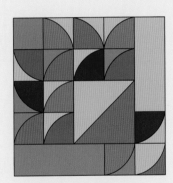

Grape Basket 47

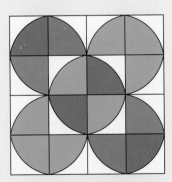

Four Leaf Clovers 48

Churn Churn Churn 49

LeAnn's Pinwheel 50

Drunkard's Path
Pattern

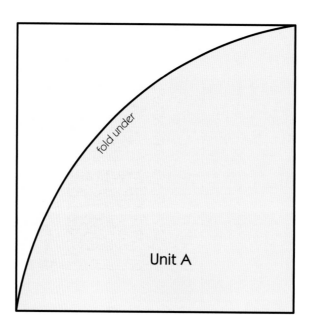

Unit A

You need extra-wide seam allowances for Piec-liqué:

> After enlarging (if desired), add a ¾" allowance around outside of the unit pattern.
> Add ⅜" allowances to inside seams, by eye, as you cut fabric pieces.

After sewing, square and trim the unit, leaving a ¼" seam allowance all around.

Sharon's Hints

▸ Use the A pattern and the layered technique to make the cornerstones for the sashing.

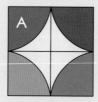

Spinning Dozen
cornerstone

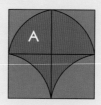

Grape Basket
cornerstone

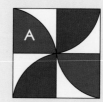

Churn Churn Churn
cornerstone

Drunkard's Path
Spinning Dozen

Technique: layered Piec-liqué, page 18

Quilt size: 76" x 76" before quilting

Block size: 12" finished

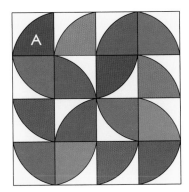

Spinning Dozen

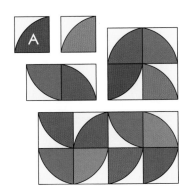

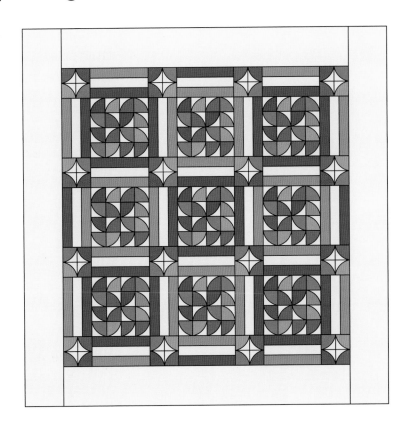

Block Resizing

9"	75%
12"	100%
15"	125%

Cutting Guide

A	unit A pattern, page 44
B	2½" x 12½" (3/sash)
C	8½" x 60½"
D	8½" x 76½"

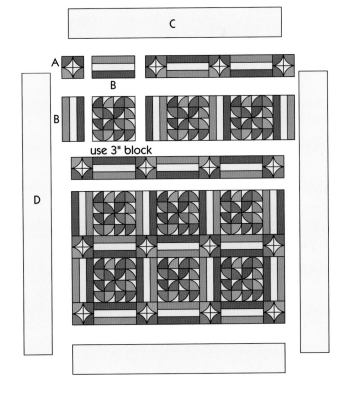

Drunkard's Path
Spring Basket

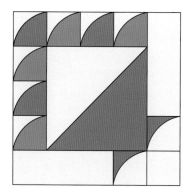

Spring Basket

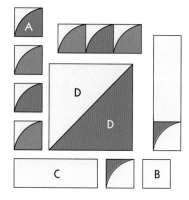

Block Resizing

9"	60%
12"	80%
15"	100%
18"	120%

Cutting Guide

A	unit A pattern, page 44
B	3½" x 3½"
C	3½" x 9½"
D	9⅞" x 9⅞" ◻
E	22½" x 22½" ⊠
F	11½" x 11½" ◻
G	1½" x 48½"
H	1½" x 50½"
I	6½" x 50½"
J	6½" x 62½"
K	2½" x 15½"
L	4" x 4" ⊠
M	2½" x 2½"

Technique: layered Piec-liqué, page 18
Quilt size: 56½" x 56½" before quilting
Block size: 15" finished

Drunkard's Path
Grape Basket

Technique: layered Piec-liqué, page 18

Quilt size: 50" x 50" before quilting

Block size: 15" finished

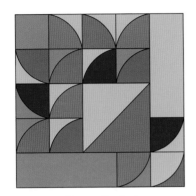

Grape Basket

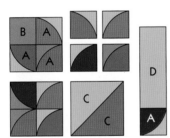

Block Resizing

9"	60%
12"	80%
15"	100%
18"	120%

Cutting Guide

A	unit A pattern, page 44
B	3½" x 3½"
C	6⅞" x 6⅞" ◻
D	3½" x 9½"
E	2½" x 15½"
F	2½" x 2½"
G	3½" x 32½"
H	3½" x 3½"
I	6½" x 38½"

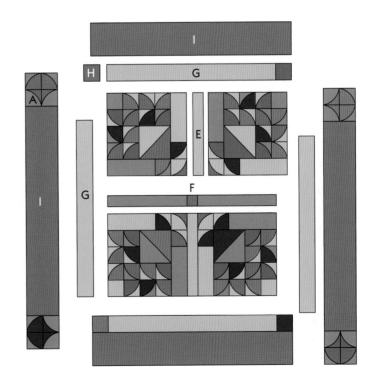

Drunkard's Path
Four Leaf Clovers

Technique: layered Piec-liqué, page 18

Quilt size: 78" x 78" before quilting

Block size: 12" finished

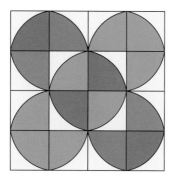

Four Leaf Clovers

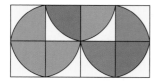

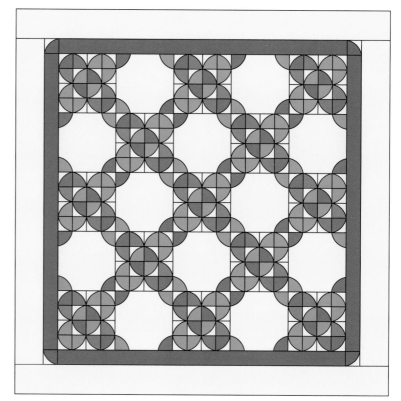

Block Resizing

9"	75%
12"	100%
15"	125%
20"	167%

Cutting Guide

A	unit A pattern, page 44
B	12½" x 12½"
C	3½" x 60½"
D	6½" x 66½"
E	6½" x 78½"

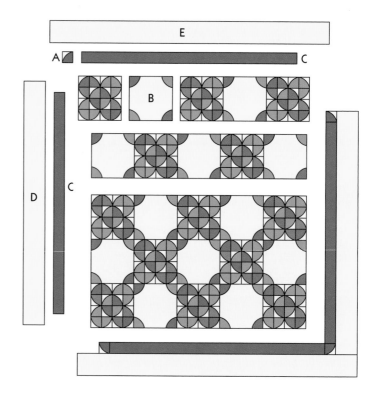

Churn Churn Churn

Technique: layered Piec-liqué, page 18

Quilt size: 93" x 93" before quilting

Block size: 18" finished

Churn Churn Churn

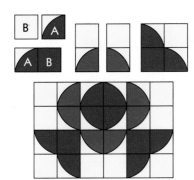

Block Resizing

12"	67%
15"	83%
18"	100%
21"	117%

Cutting Guide

A	unit A pattern, page 44
B	3½" x 3½"
C	6½" x 18½"
D	2" x 78½"
E	2" x 2"
F	3½" x 81½"
G	3½" x 87½"
H	3½" x 93½"

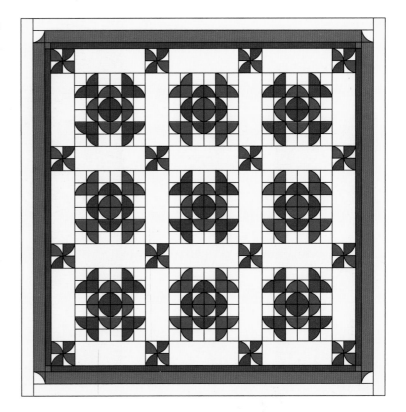

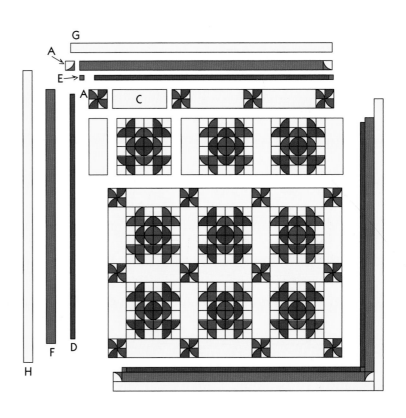

Drunkard's Path
LeAnn's Pinwheel

Technique: layered Piec-liqué, page 18
Quilt size: 87" x 87" before quilting
Block size: 15" finished

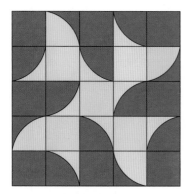

LeAnn's Star

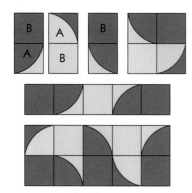

Block Resizing

9"	60%
12"	80%
15"	100%
18"	120%

Cutting Guide

A	unit A pattern, page 44
B	3½" x 3½"
C	3½" x 15½"
D	3½" x 9½"
E	3½" x 3½"
F	6½" x 75½"
G	6½" x 87½"

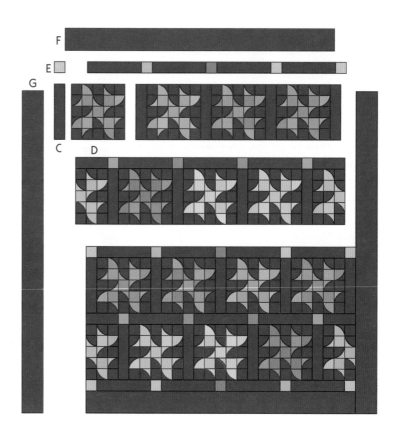

Grandma's Fan

Technique: layered Piec-liqué, page 18
Quilt size: 68" x 68" before quilting
Block size: 8" finished

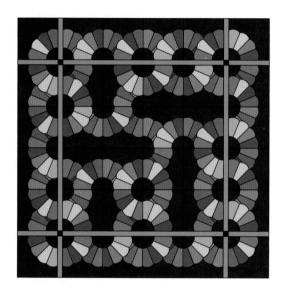

Alternate quilt layout

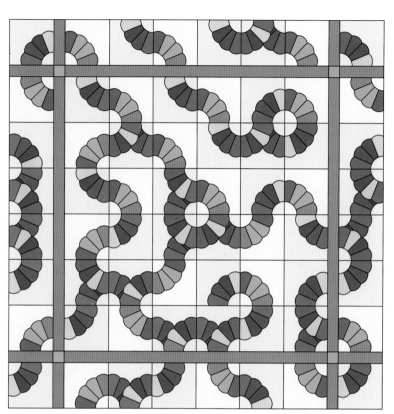

block A   **block B**

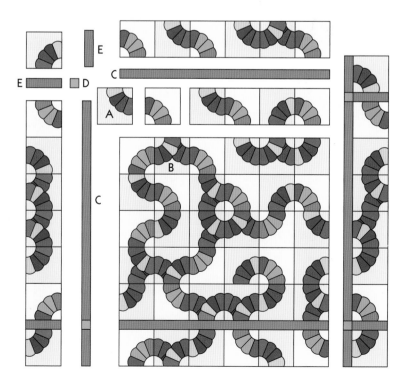

Cutting Guide

A   block A pattern, page 52
    enlarge 134%

B   block B pattern
    page 53, enlarge 134%

C   2½" x 48½"

D   2½" x 2½"

E   2½"" x 8½"

Grandma's Fan A Pattern

Enlarge 134% for 68" x 68" quilt.

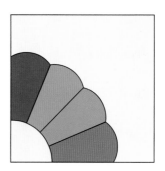

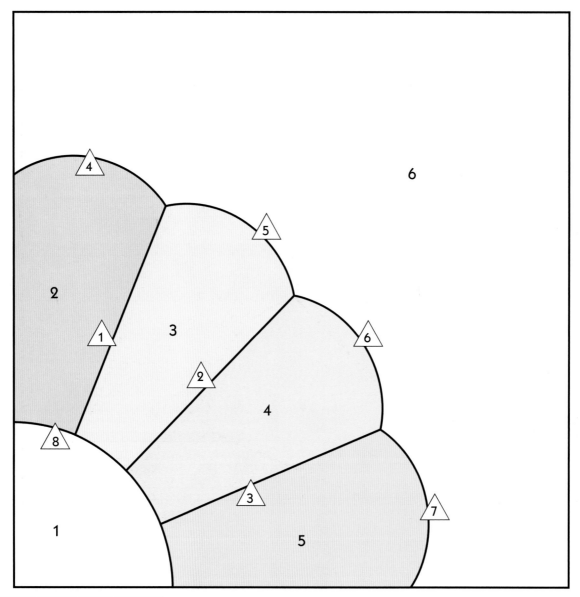

Block Resizing

6"	100%
8"	134%
10"	167%
12"	200%
14"	233%
16"	267%

Piece numbers = layering order
Numbers in triangles = sewing sequence for seams
You need extra-wide seam allowances for Piec-liqué:
    After enlarging (if desired), add a ¾" allowance around outside of the block pattern.
     Add ⅜" allowances to inside seams, by eye, as you cut fabric pieces.
After sewing, square and trim the block, leaving a ¼" seam allowance all around.

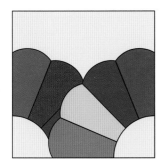

Grandma's Fan B Pattern

Enlarge 134% for 68" x 68" quilt.

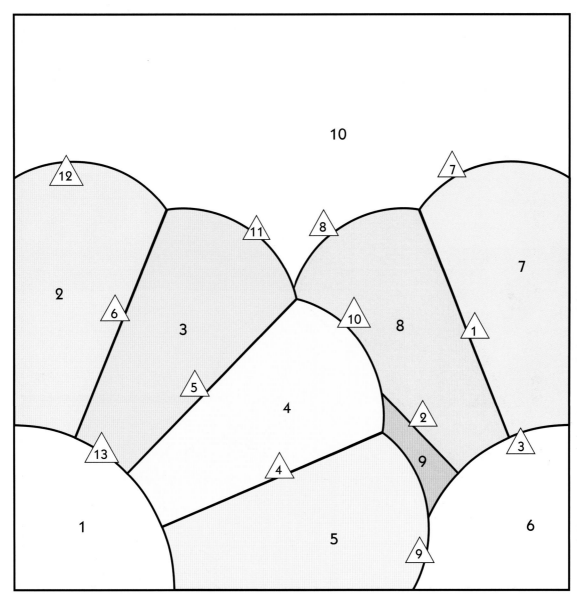

Block Resizing

6"	100%
8"	134%
10"	167%
12"	200%
14"	233%
16"	267%

Piece numbers = layering order
Numbers in triangles = sewing sequence for seams
You need extra-wide seam allowances for Piec-liqué:
  After enlarging (if desired), add a ¾" allowance around outside of the block pattern.
  Add ⅜" allowances to inside seams, by eye, as you cut fabric pieces.
After sewing, square and trim the block, leaving a ¼" seam allowance all around.

Lazy Daisy design by Cristy Atkin

Technique: layered Piec-liqué, page 18
Quilt size: 40" x 40" before quilting
Block size: 6" finished

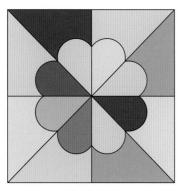

Block Unit

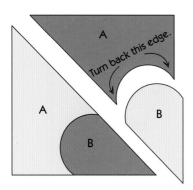

Cutting Guide

A   block pattern, page 55
B   1½" x 24½"
C   1½" x 26½"
D   6½" x 39¼"
E   1½" x 38½"
F   1½" x 40½"

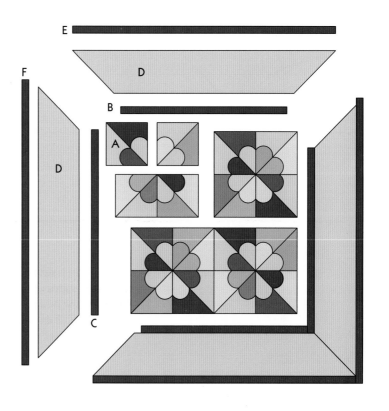

Lazy Daisy Pattern

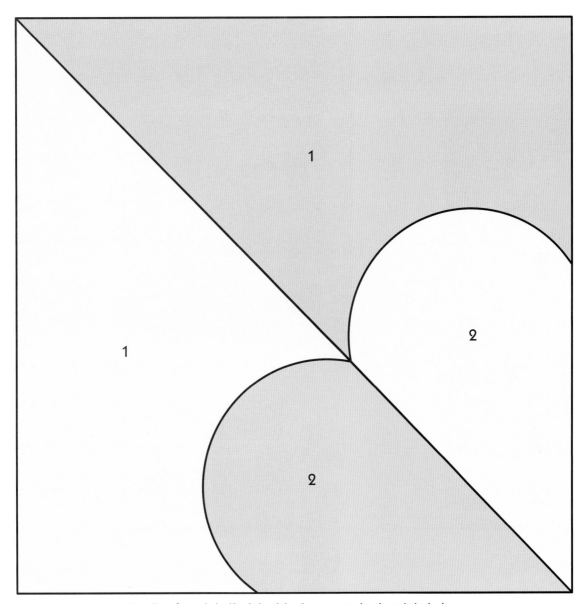

Piec-liqué each half of the block separately, then join halves.

Block Resizing

6"	100%
8"	134%
10"	167%
12"	200%
14"	233%
16"	267%

Piece numbers = layering order
You need extra-wide seam allowances for Piec-liqué:
    After enlarging (if desired), add a ¾" allowance around outside of the block pattern.
    Add ⅜" allowances to inside seams, by eye, as you cut fabric pieces.
After sewing, square and trim the block, leaving a ¼" seam allowance all around.

New York Beauty

Techniques: layered Piec-liqué, page 18
foundation piecing, page 59

Quilt size: 96" x 96" before quilting

Block size: 12" finished

New York Beauty

New York Beauty Border

Cutting Guide

A   block A pattern
page 57, enlarge 200%

B   block B pattern
page 58, enlarge 200%

C   half block pattern
page 58, enlarge 200%

New York Beauty A Pattern

Enlarge 200% for 96" x 96" quilt.

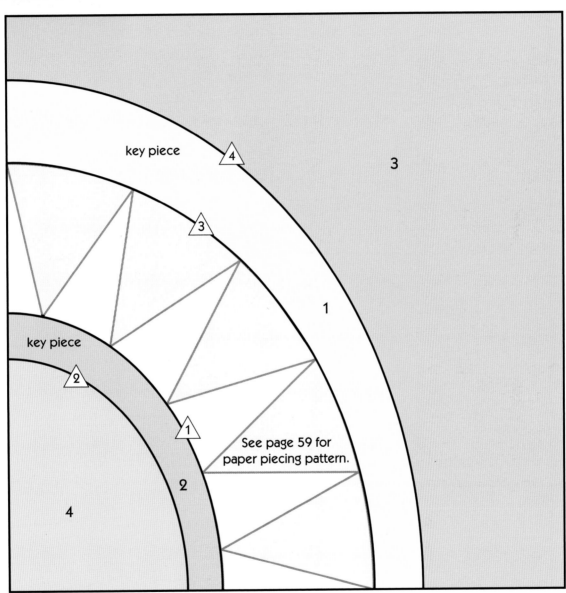

key piece

4

3

3

1

key piece

2

1

2

See page 59 for
paper piecing pattern.

4

Block Resizing

6"	100%
8"	134%
10"	167%
12"	200%
14"	233%
16"	267%

Piece numbers = layering order
Numbers in triangles = sewing sequence for seams
You need extra-wide seam allowances for Piec-liqué:
　　After enlarging (if desired), add a ¾" allowance around outside of the block pattern.
　　Add ⅜" allowances to inside seams, by eye, as you cut fabric pieces.
After sewing, square and trim the block, leaving a ¼" seam allowance all around.

New York Beauty B Pattern

Enlarge 200% for 96" x 96" quilt.

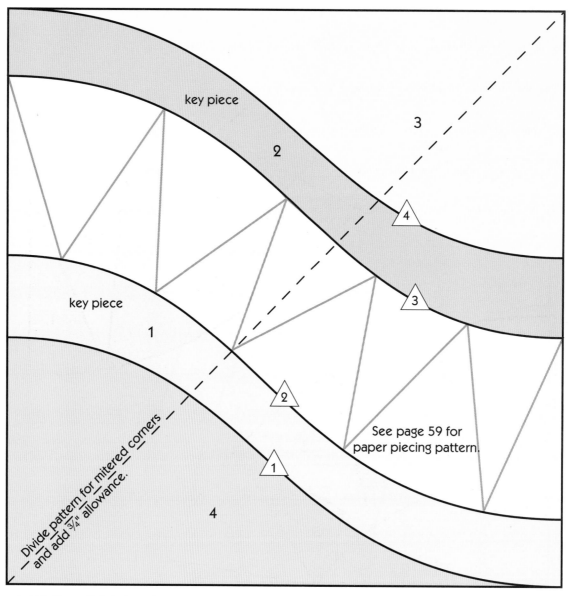

key piece

3

2

4

key piece

1

3

2

Divide pattern for mitered corners
and add ¾" allowance.

1

See page 59 for
paper piecing pattern.

4

Block Resizing

6"	100%
8"	134%
10"	167%
12"	200%
14"	233%
16"	267%

Piece numbers = layering order
Numbers in triangles = sewing sequence for seams
You need extra-wide seam allowances for Piec-liqué:
    After enlarging (if desired), add a ¾" allowance around outside of the block pattern.
    Add ⅜" allowances to inside seams, by eye, as you cut fabric pieces.
After sewing, square and trim the block, leaving a ¼" seam allowance all around.

New York Beauty paper piecing patterns

Enlarge 200% for 96" x 96" quilt.

▶ After enlarging (if desired), add a ⅜" allowance around outside of the block pattern.

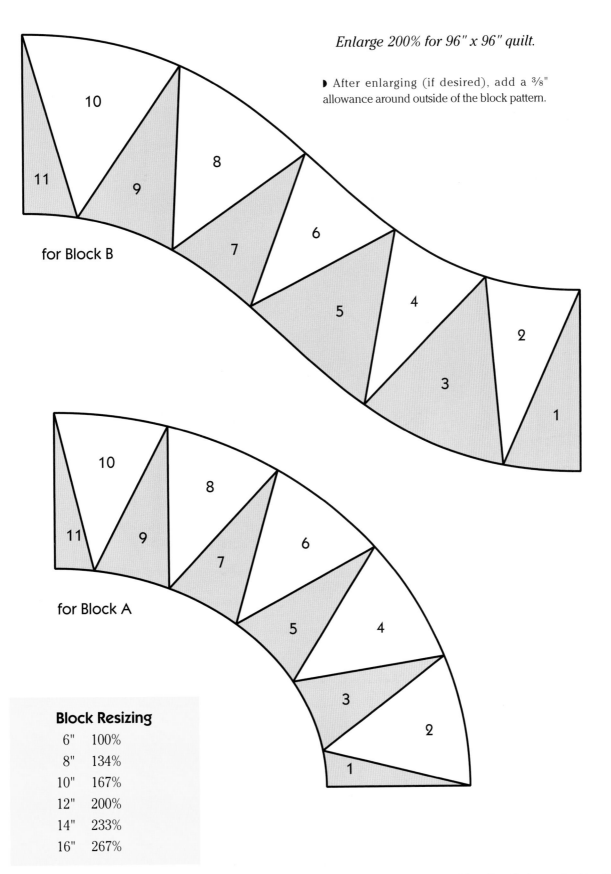

for Block B

for Block A

Block Resizing

6"	100%
8"	134%
10"	167%
12"	200%
14"	233%
16"	267%

Tile Floor

Technique: layered Piec-liqué, page 18
free-form Piec-liqué, page 27
Quilt size: 57" x 57" before quilting
Block size: 6" finished

Tile Floor block 61

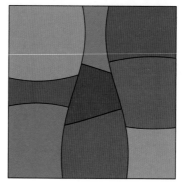

Broken Tile block 32

Tile Floor Pattern

You can use the Broken Tile blocks (page 32) to make 20 A and 16 B blocks.

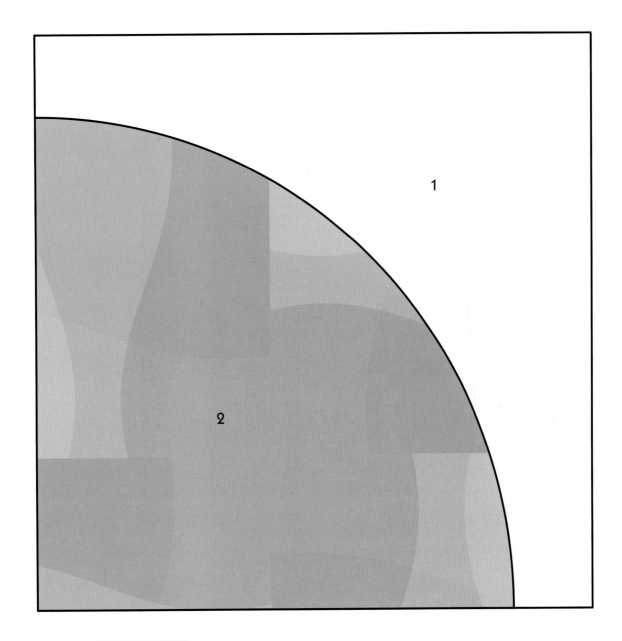

Block Resizing

6"	100%
8"	134%
10"	167%
12"	200%
14"	233%
16"	267%

Piece numbers = layering order
You need extra-wide seam allowances for Piec-liqué:
    After enlarging (if desired), add a ¾" allowance around outside of the block pattern.
    Add ⅜" allowances to inside seams, by eye, as you cut fabric pieces.
After sewing, square and trim the block, leaving a ¼" seam allowance all around.

Tile Floor

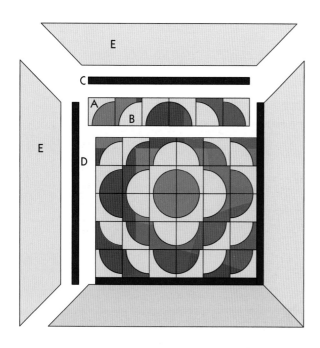

Cutting Guide

A   TILE FLOOR pattern page 61
B   TILE FLOOR pattern, reverse colors
C   2" x 36½"
D   2½" x 39½"
E   9½" x 58¼"

Sharon's Hints

Making Serpentine Borders

▸ Join the blocks and add all the borders before making the serpentine cuts in the borders. Working with one side of the quilt at a time, free-form serpentine cut the outer border (fig. 1).

▸ Using the half-circle border pattern from Shooting Marbles, page 42, cut the desired number of half circles. (Add a ⅜" allowance to the fabric circles.)

▸ Randomly set the half circles along both sides of the serpentine cut (fig. 2). Use the layered technique to sew them to the border. Press.

▸ Cut 1½" wide purple bias strips. Sew them together, end to end, as needed to make four strips 60" long. Be sure to starch the strips well and turn both long edges.

▸ With all pieces right side up, realign the raw edges of the serpentine cut so they just touch. Glue a bias strip on top, following the curves and overlapping both sides of the cut border. Sew in the fold and press (fig. 3). Repeat for the other three sides of the quilt.

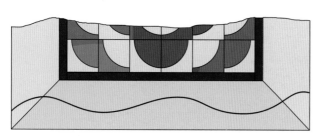

Fig. 1

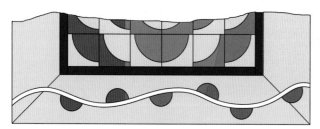

Fig. 2

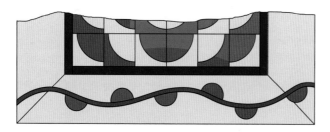

Fig. 3

Sew Sweet Basket

Technique: inset Piec-liqué, page 14
                  layered Piec-liqué, page 18

Quilt size: 60" x 60" before quilting

Block size: 14" finished

Cutting Guide

A   basket pattern, page 64, enlarge 233%

B   daisy pattern, page 65, enlarge 233%

C   sashing pattern, page 66, enlarge 233%

D   half sashing pattern, enlarge 233%

E   cornerstone pattern, enlarge 233%

F   8¼" x 8¼"

G   8¼" x 45¾"

    (G is extra long for ensurance.)

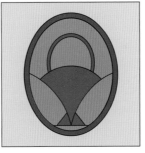

Sew Sweet Basket 64

Sew Sweet Daisy 65

Sew Sweet Basket basket block

Enlarge 233% for 60" x 60" quilt.

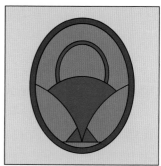

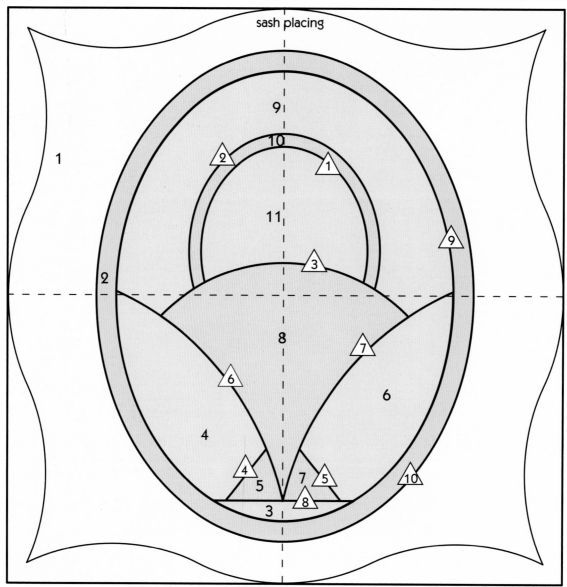

Block Resizing

6"	100%
8"	134%
10"	167%
12"	200%
14"	233%
16"	267%

Piece numbers = layering order

Numbers in triangles = sewing sequence for seams

You need extra-wide seam allowances for Piec-liqué:

    After enlarging (if desired), add a ¾" allowance around outside of the block pattern.

    Add ⅜" allowances to inside seams, by eye, as you cut fabric pieces.

After sewing, square and trim the block, leaving a ¼" seam allowance all around.

Sew Sweet Basket Daisy block

Enlarge 233% for 60" x 60" quilt.

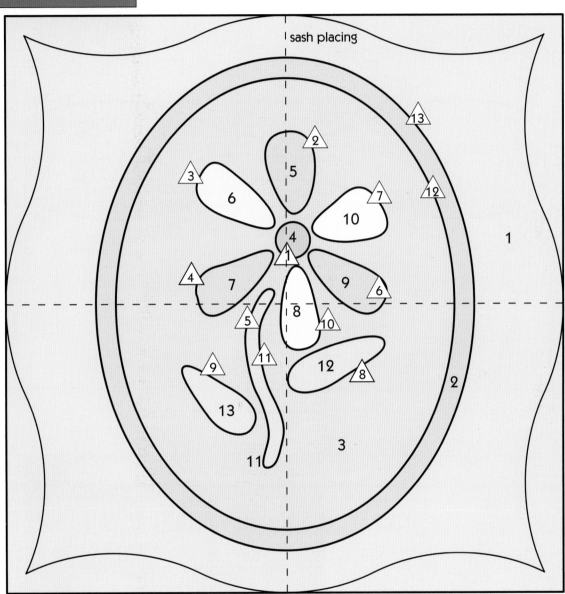

Block Resizing

6"	100%
8"	134%
10"	167%
12"	200%
14"	233%
16"	267%

Piece numbers = layering order
Numbers in triangles = sewing sequence for seams
You need extra-wide seam allowances for Piec-liqué:
    After enlarging (if desired), add a ¾" allowance around outside of the block pattern.
    Add ⅜" allowances to inside seams, by eye, as you cut fabric pieces.
After sewing, square and trim the block, leaving a ¼" seam allowance all around.

Sew Sweet Basket sashing patterns

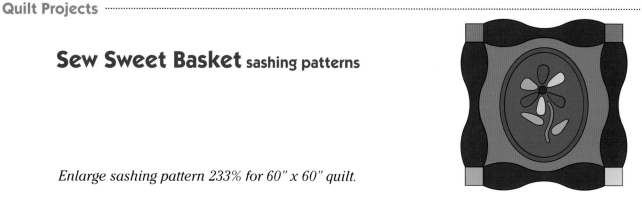

Enlarge sashing pattern 233% for 60" x 60" quilt.

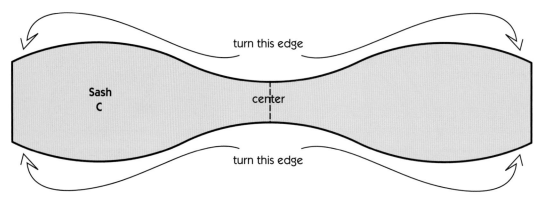

turn this edge

Sash
C

center

turn this edge

Split on dashed line for corner sashing.

Sashing
Cornerstone

Block Resizing

6"	100%
8"	134%
10"	167%
12"	200%
14"	233%
16"	267%

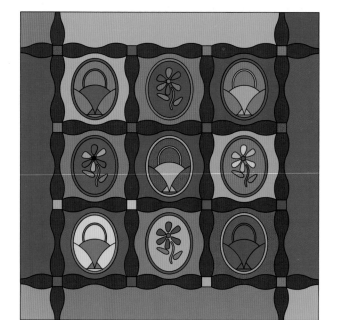

Sew Sweet Basket

Sharon's Hints

Adding Sashing

▶ Refer to the technique used for the Broken Tile block, page 32. Turn all the long edges of the sashes. Do not turn the ends. Turn under all four edges for each cornerstone.

▶ Using the placement guide, align two vertical sashes between three blocks to make each block row (fig. 1). Glue and heat-set in position. Sew in the fold and press.

▶ Glue and press two cornerstones between three horizontal sashes, as shown, to make the sash rows. Sew and press.

▶ Align the sash rows with the block rows. Glue and press, making sure that you maintain the alignment. Sew and press the sashes.

▶ Repeat the process for the border, following the assembly diagram (fig. 2).

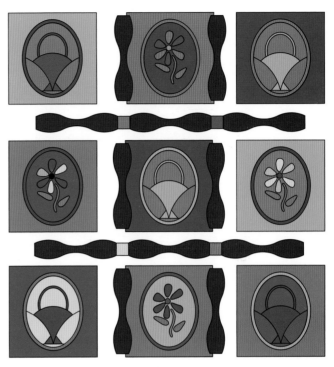

Fig. 1

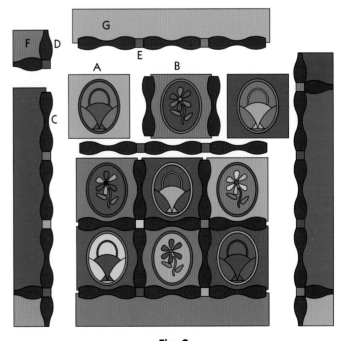

Fig. 2

Gumball Quilt

Technique: inset Piec-liqué, page 14
layered Piec-liqué, page 18

Quilt size: 47" x 47" before quilting

Block size: 6" finished

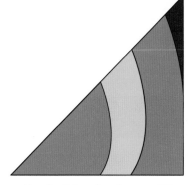

Gumball Border Corner 70

Gumball Border 70

Corner Flower 71

Gumball Block Pattern

Cutting Guide

A   Gumball pattern, this page
B   Flower pattern, page 71
C   border pattern, page 70
D   border corner pattern, page 70
E   20⅞" x 20⅞"
F   1¼" x 21½"
G   1¼" x 22"
H   2¾" x 26½"
I   2¾" x 24½"

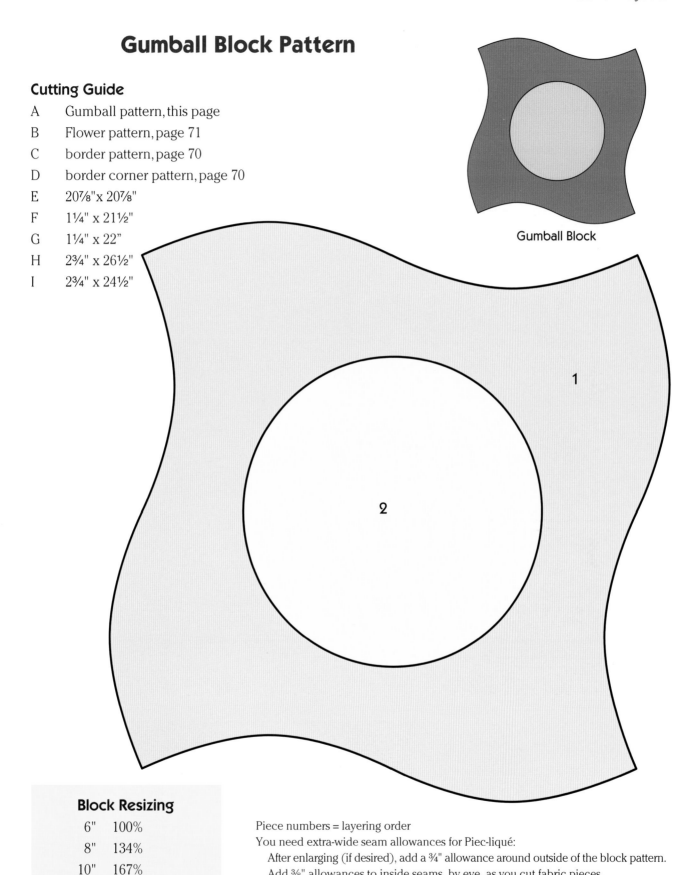

Gumball Block

Block Resizing	
6"	100%
8"	134%
10"	167%
12"	200%
14"	233%

Piece numbers = layering order
You need extra-wide seam allowances for Piec-liqué:
   After enlarging (if desired), add a ¾" allowance around outside of the block pattern.
   Add ⅜" allowances to inside seams, by eye, as you cut fabric pieces.
After sewing, square and trim the block, leaving a ¼" seam allowance all around.

Gumball Quilt border pattern

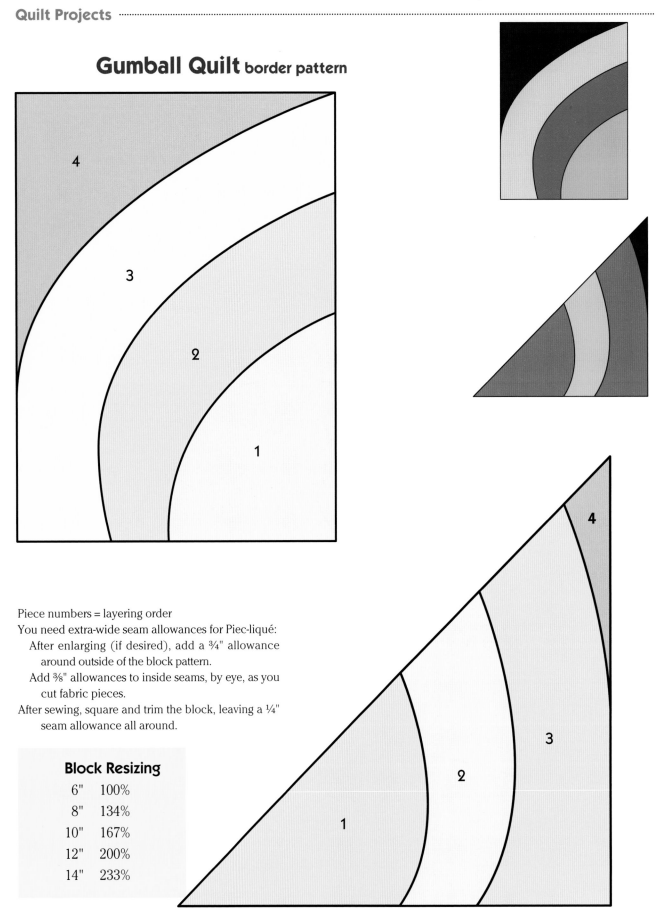

Piece numbers = layering order

You need extra-wide seam allowances for Piec-liqué:

After enlarging (if desired), add a ¾" allowance
around outside of the block pattern.

Add ⅜" allowances to inside seams, by eye, as you
cut fabric pieces.

After sewing, square and trim the block, leaving a ¼"
seam allowance all around.

Block Resizing

6"	100%
8"	134%
10"	167%
12"	200%
14"	233%

Gumball Quilt corner flower pattern

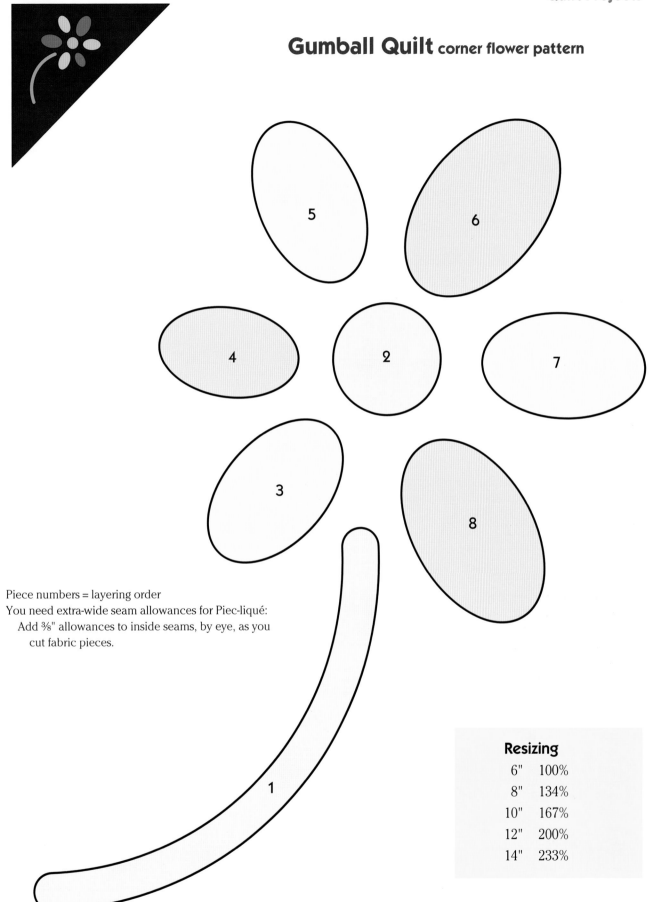

Piece numbers = layering order
You need extra-wide seam allowances for Piec-liqué:
  Add ⅜" allowances to inside seams, by eye, as you
  cut fabric pieces.

Resizing

6"	100%
8"	134%
10"	167%
12"	200%
14"	233%

Gumball Quilt

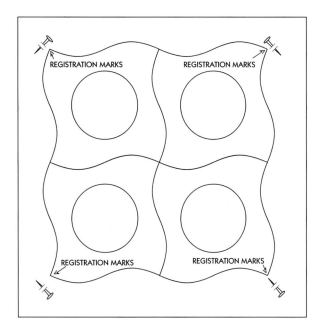

Fig. 1

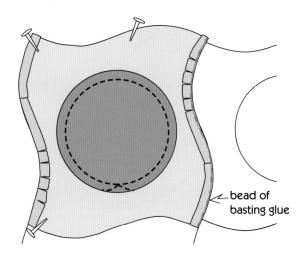

Fig. 2

bead of
basting glue

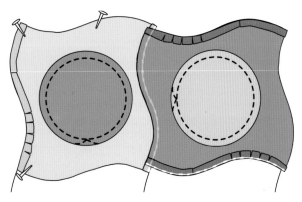

Fig. 3

Sharon's Hints

Assembling Blocks

▶ After making all the Gumball blocks, prepare a placement guide that includes four blocks set two by two. Pin the guide to your pressing mat (fig. 1).

▶ Starch and turn the edges on two opposite sides of every Gumball block. Secure the first block to the mat with pins. If the block has become distorted, press it into shape.

▶ Place a thin line of glue along the fold of the first seam, as shown in red in figure 2. Before the glue dries, place the next block on top, aligning one of its raw edges with the folded edge underneath. (fig. 3). Press dry to heat-set.

▶ Take the blocks off the guide. Position them to expose the fold line. Sew along the fold, beginning and ending at the cross-seam folds so that the seam allowances remain unsewn (fig. 4).

▶ Return the blocks to the guide and continue the same process to complete a four-block set. Check to make sure that all the points line up. Make four sets like this. In the same manner, make four two-block sets. You will have a single block left.

▶ Using a permanent pen, put small tick marks at the corners of each set, as shown in figure 5. Using these registration marks to align the sets, join the four-block and two block sets, along with the single block (fig. 6).

Gumball Quilt

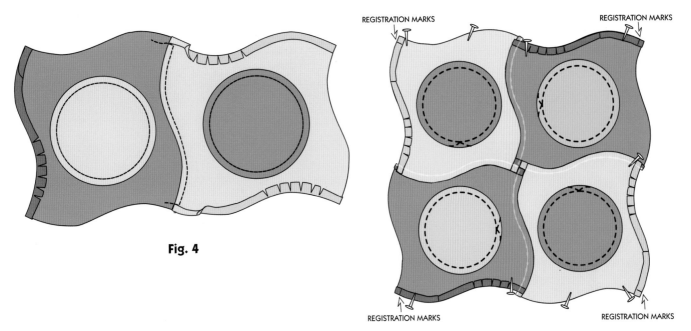

Fig. 4

Fig. 5

Fig. 6

French Country

Technique: inset Piec-liqué, page 14
layered Piec-liqué, page 18

Quilt size: 74" x 74" before quilting

Finished Block size:

Center flower block   28"

Border Flower block   14"

Cornerstones   5"

French Country Block

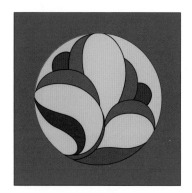

Cornerstone Block

Cutting Guide

A French Country block pattern
page 75, enlarge 467%

B French Country block pattern
page 75, enlarge 233%

C cornerstones pattern
page 76

D 4½" x 28½"

E 5½" x 28½"

F 4½" x 56½"

G 4½" x 64½"

H 5½" x 64½"

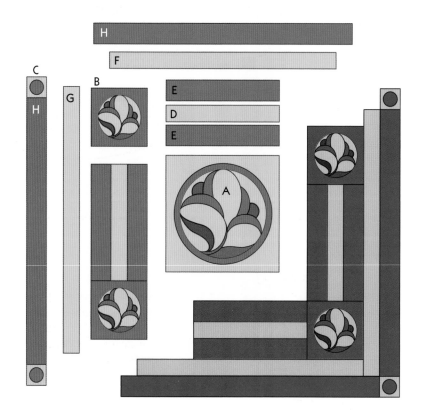

French Country Pattern

For 74" x 74" quilt, enlarge 467% for 28" center flower and 233% for border flower.

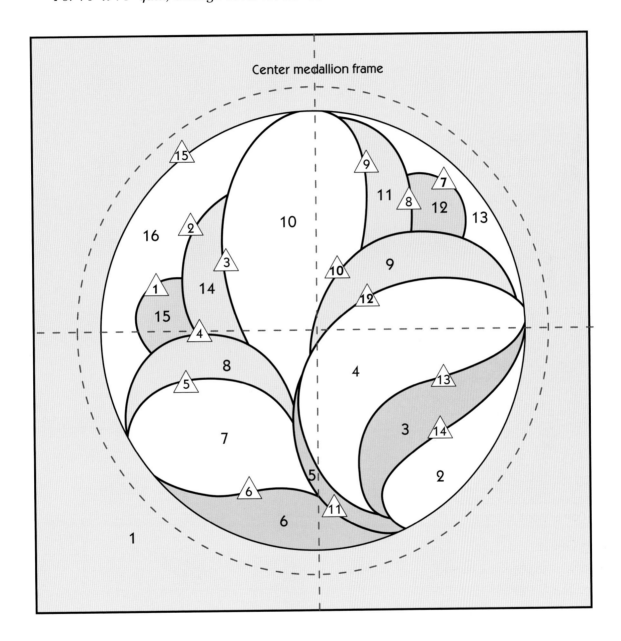

Center medallion frame

Block Resizing

8"	134%
10"	167%
12"	200%
14"	233%
16"	267%
28"	467%

Piece numbers = layering order

Numbers in triangles = sewing sequence for seams

You need extra-wide seam allowances for Piec-liqué:

    After enlarging (if desired), add a ¾" allowance around outside of the block pattern.

    Add ⅜" allowances to inside seams, by eye, as you cut fabric pieces.

After sewing, square and trim the block, leaving a ¼" seam allowance all around.

French Country Cornerstone Block

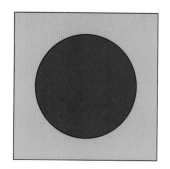

Use at this 5" size for a 74" x 74" quilt.

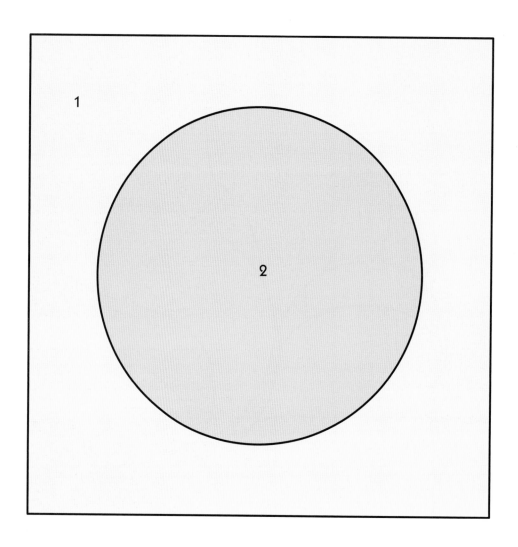

Block Resizing

8"	134%
10"	167%
12"	200%
14"	233%
16"	267%
28"	467%

Piece numbers = layering order
You need extra-wide seam allowances for Piec-liqué:
    After enlarging (if desired), add a ¾" allowance around outside of the block pattern.
    Add ⅜" allowances to inside seams, by eye, as you cut fabric pieces.
After sewing, square and trim the block, leaving a ¼" seam allowance all around.

Traditional Marble Quilt (patterns on pages 78–79)

Technique: inset Piec-liqué, page 14
free-form Piec-liqué, page 27

Quilt size: 69" x 77½" before quilting

Block size: 6" finished

Shooting Marble Block

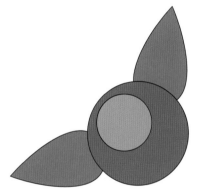

Traditional Marble Border

Cutting Guide

A   Shooting Marble block
pattern, page 78

B   border flower pattern
page 79

C   9¾" x 9¾"   ⊠

D   5⅛" x 5⅛"   ◻

E   9½" x 60"

F   9½" x 69½"

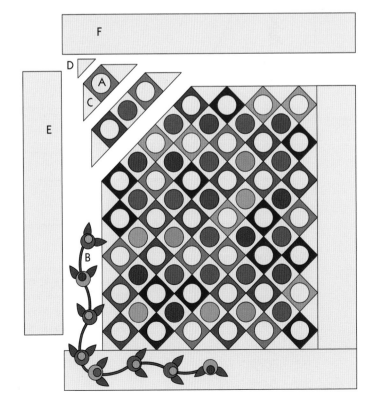

Traditional Marble Quilt Shooting Marble Block

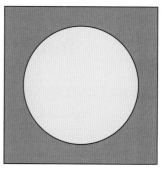

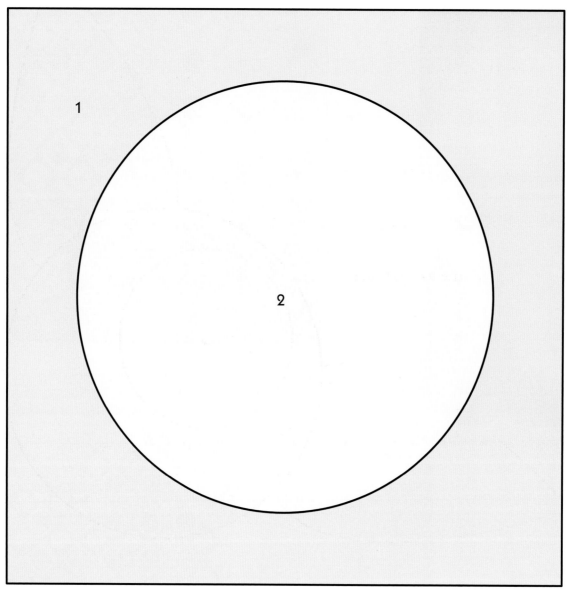

1

2

Block Resizing

6"	100%
8"	134%
10"	167%
12"	200%
14"	233%
16"	267%

Piece numbers = layering order
You need extra-wide seam allowances for Piec-liqué:
    After enlarging (if desired), add a ¾" allowance around outside of the block pattern.
    Add ⅜" allowances to inside seams, by eye, as you cut fabric pieces.
After sewing, square and trim the block, leaving a ¼" seam allowance all around.

Traditional Marble Quilt Border Flower

Sharon's Hints

▶ Use the free-form technique for the vine in the border (see Making Serpentine Borders, page 62) and use the inset and layering techniques for the border flowers.

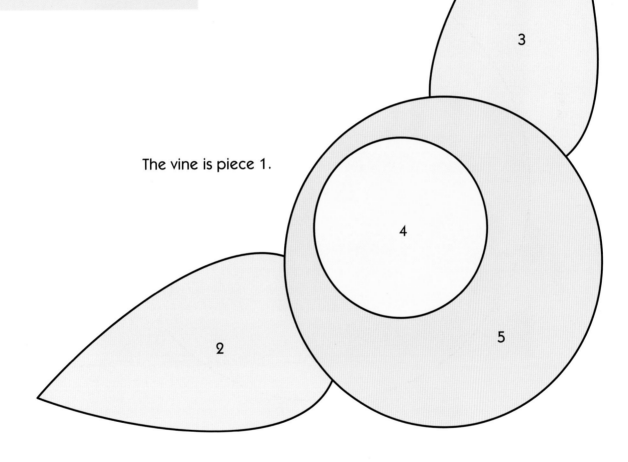

The vine is piece 1.

Resizing

6"	100%
8"	134%
10"	167%
12"	200%
14"	233%
16"	267%

Piece numbers = layering order
You need extra-wide seam allowances for Piec-liqué:
   Add ⅜" allowances to inside seams, by eye, as you cut fabric pieces.

Swimming Free

Technique: inset Piec-liqué, page 14

free-form Piec-liqué, page 27

Quilt size: 26" x 26" before quilting

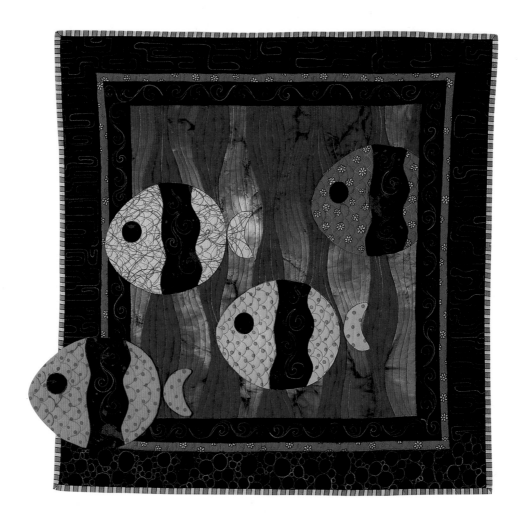

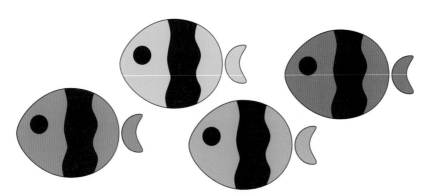

Swimming Free blocks

Swimming Free

Enlarge 150% for 28" x 28" quilt.

See page 82 for background (center panel) assembly.
See page 83–84 for fish assembly.

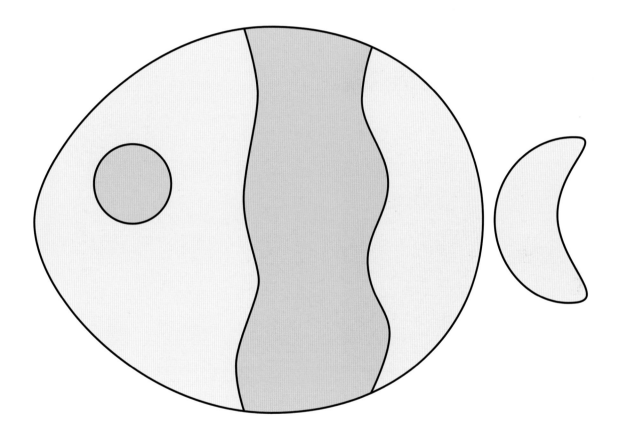

You need extra-wide seam allowances for Piec-liqué:
  After enlarging (if desired), add a ¾" allowance around outside of the block pattern.
  Add ⅜" allowances to inside seams, by eye, as you cut fabric pieces.

Swimming Free

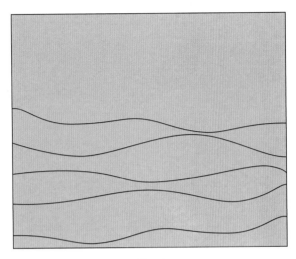

Fig. 1

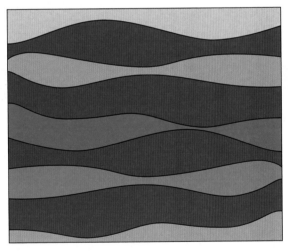

Fig. 2

Sharon's Hints

Making Waves

▶ Select five fat quarters for the water. Lay the five fat quarters on top of each other, all right side up. Free-form serpentine cut half of the stack, as shown in figure 1. You can cut more strips if needed. Starch and turn the top edge of each strip.

▶ Arrange the strips in a pleasing manner, as shown in figure 2. After you have organized the strips the way you want, glue and heat-set the seams. Continue to add pieces until the center panel is larger than 20" by 20". Sew and press all the seams. Trim the center panel to 18½" x 18½".

Swimming Free

Sharon's Hints

Making Fish

▶ Cut a 10" square for each fish. To make the black, wavy stripe in the fish, serpentine cut through the center of the 10" square. Turn the serpentine edges back on both pieces (fig. 3).

▶ Cut a 3½" x 10" black strip. Place both serpentine-cut pieces on the black strip, leaving an area of black showing (fig. 4). Glue, heat-set, and sew in the fold to complete the fish fabric.

▶ Make a template for the eye. Place the fish pattern on the fish fabric to find the eye placement (fig. 5). Then use the inset technique to sew the eye in the fish fabric.

*Be sure to put templates on the **wrong sides** of the fabrics.*

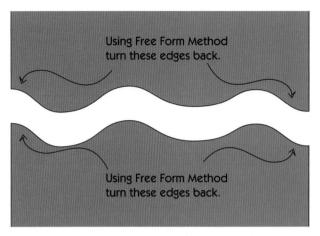

Fig. 3

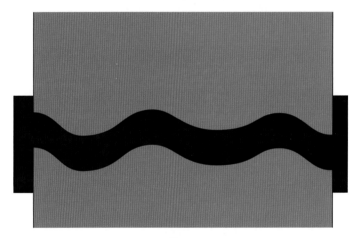

Fig. 4

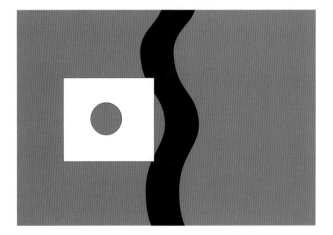

Fig. 5

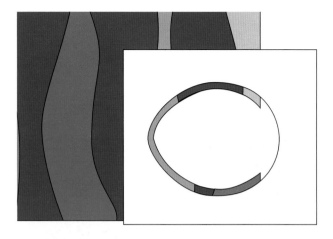

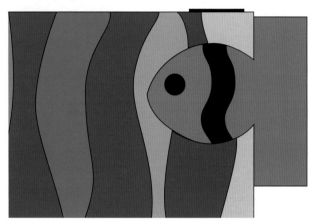

Fig. 6

▶ Make a template for the fish body and tail. Use the inset technique to sew these pieces in the waves (fig. 6). Press the seam allowances toward the fish.

Swimming-Free Fish

▶ Sew the border strips to the quilt top then use the inset technique to add fish that are partially in the water and partially in the border.

▶ After quilting the layers and binding the edges of the quilt, make any fish that extend beyond the borders as if they were little pillows and appliqué them to the quilt.

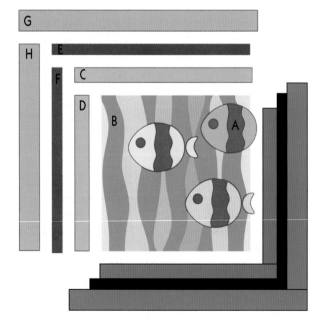

Cutting Guide

A	fish pattern, page 81, enlarge 150%
B	center panel, trim to 18½" x 18½"
C	1¾" x 20½"
D	1¾" x 23"
E	1¼" x 23"
F	1¼" x 24½"
G	2½" x 24½"
H	2½" x 28½"

More Block Patterns

Sunrise 86

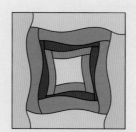

Spinning Square 87

Black-Eyed Susan 88

Susie Q 89

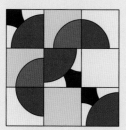

Delicate Doves 90

Too Many Daisies 91

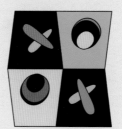

Tic Tac Toe 92

Magic Flame 94

Blue Bells in My Garden 95

Quiet Dreams 96

Wild Rose 97

Dove of Peace 98

Morning Breeze 99

Crimson Iris 100

Piece numbers = layering order
Numbers in triangles = sewing sequence for seams
You need extra-wide seam allowances for Piec-liqué:
    After enlarging (if desired), add a ¾" allowance around out-
        side of the block pattern.
    Add ⅜" allowances to inside seams, by eye, as you cut
        fabric pieces.
After sewing, square and trim the block, leaving a ¼" seam
        allowance all around.

Sunrise

Technique: layered Piec-liqué, page 18

Block size: 6" finished

Block Resizing	
6"	100%
8"	134%
10"	167%
12"	200%
14"	233%
16"	267%

Sharon's Hints

▶ Make a paper foundation template for the sunrays.

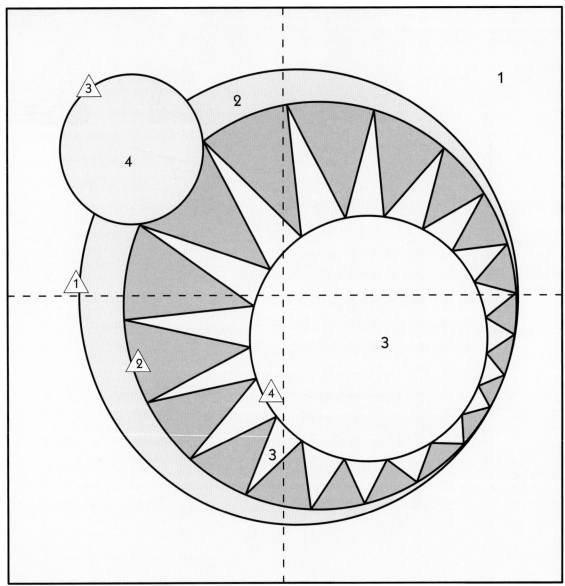

Spinning Square

Technique: split-seam Piec-liqué, page 23

Block size: 6" finished

Block Resizing

6"	100%
8"	134%
10"	167%
12"	200%
14"	233%
16"	267%

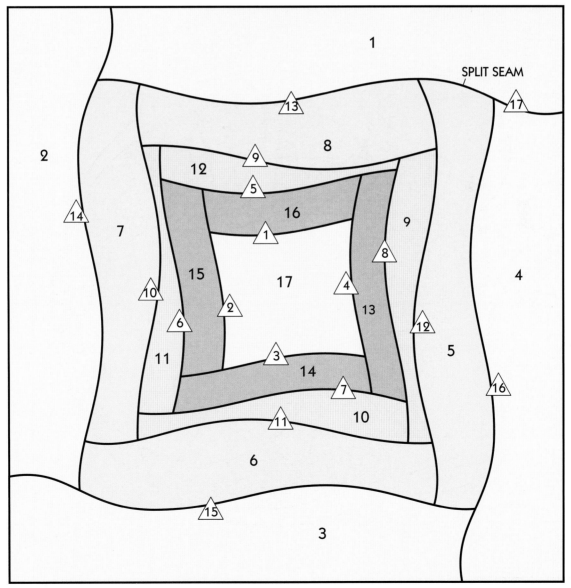

Black-Eyed Susan

Technique: layered Piec-liqué, page 18
Block size: 6" finished

Block Resizing

25"	418%
30"	500%
35"	580%
40"	665%

Quilt shown on page 102.

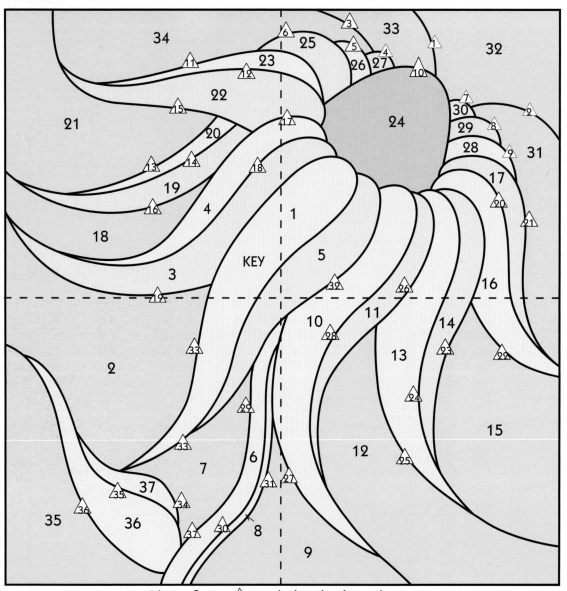

Note: Seam ⚠33 encircles the key piece.

Susie Q

Technique: layered Piec-liqué
page 18

Block size: 4⅝" x 9½" finished

15

16

△1
△2
△3
13
12
△4
8
△8
11
△5
10
△6
7
9
△7
△13
6
5
2
4
△9
14
KeyIPiece
△14
△20
△11
1
△12
3
△10

split seam

20
△18
△16
21
△17
△15
18
19
22
△19
17
△21

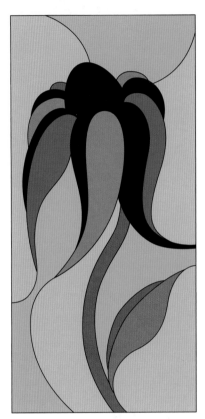

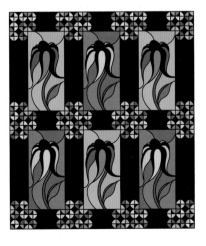

Quilt shown on page 103.

Delicate Doves

Technique: layered Piec-liqué, page 18
Block size: 12" finished

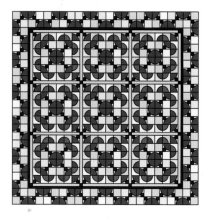

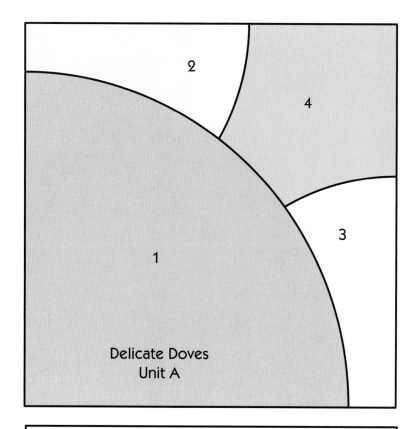

Delicate Doves
Unit A

Delicate Doves
Unit B

Block Resizing	
6"	50%
8"	67%
10"	83.5%
12"	100%
14"	116.5%
16"	134%

Too Many Daisies

Technique: inset Piec-liqué, page 14
Block size: approx. 5¾" x 7" finished

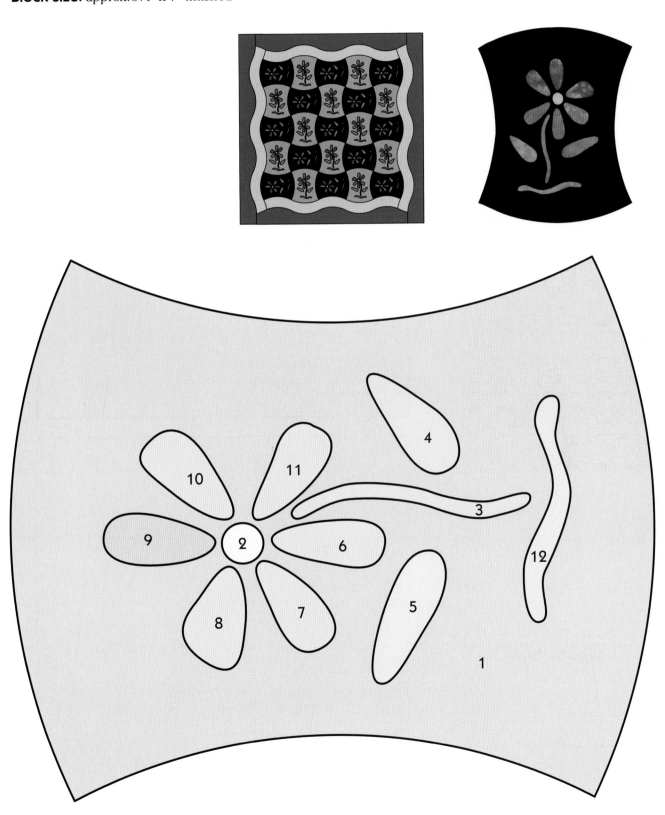

Tic Tac Toe

Technique: inset Piec-liqué, page 14
Block size: 6" finished

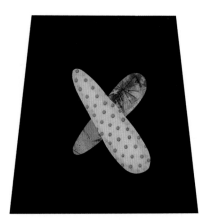

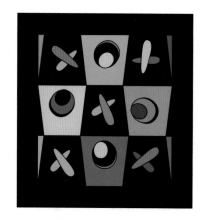

Block Resizing

6"	100%
8"	134%
10"	167%
12"	200%
14"	233%
16"	267%

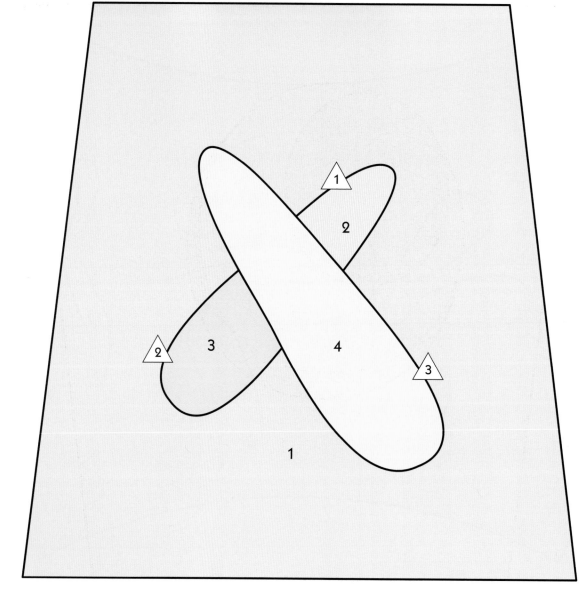

Tic Tac Toe

Technique: inset Piec-liqué, page 14

Block size: 6" finished

Block Resizing

6"	100%
8"	134%
10"	167%
12"	200%
14"	233%
16"	267%

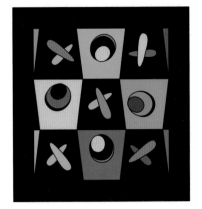

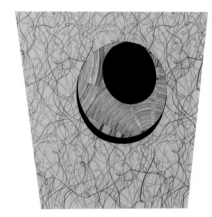

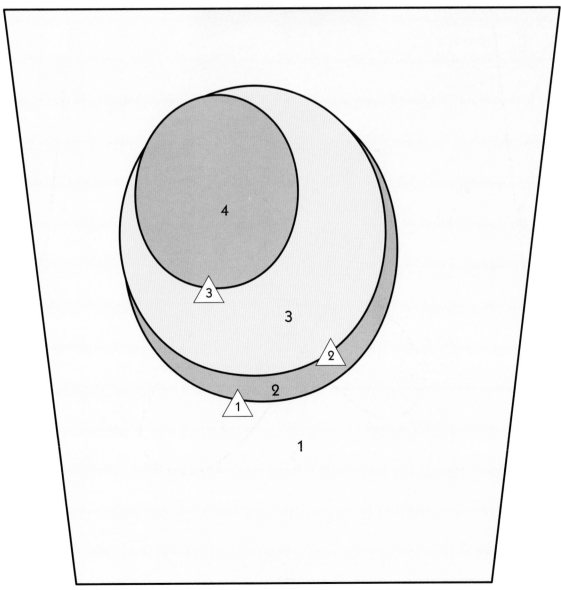

Magic Flame

Technique: layered Piec-liqué, page 18
Block size: 6" finished

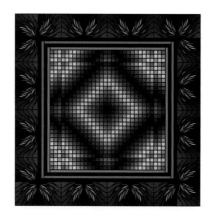

Block Resizing

6"	100%
8"	134%
10"	167%
12"	200%
14"	233%
16"	267%

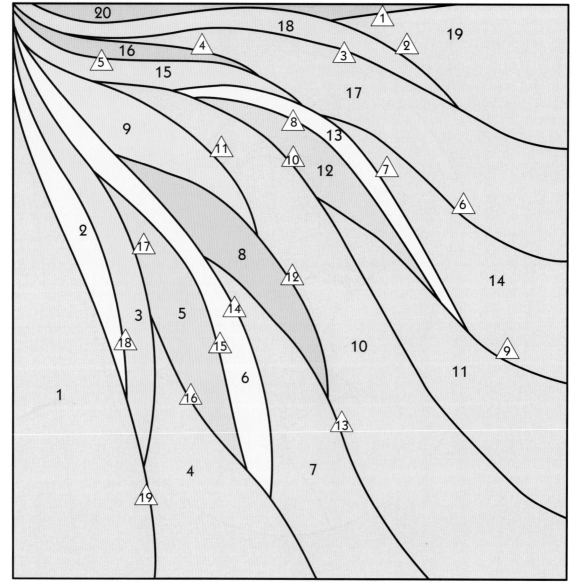

Blue Bells in My Garden

Technique: inset Piec-liqué, page 14

layered Piec-liqué, page 18

Block size: 6" finished

Block Resizing

6"	100%
8"	134%
10"	167%
12"	200%
14"	233%
16"	267%

Quilt shown on page 104.

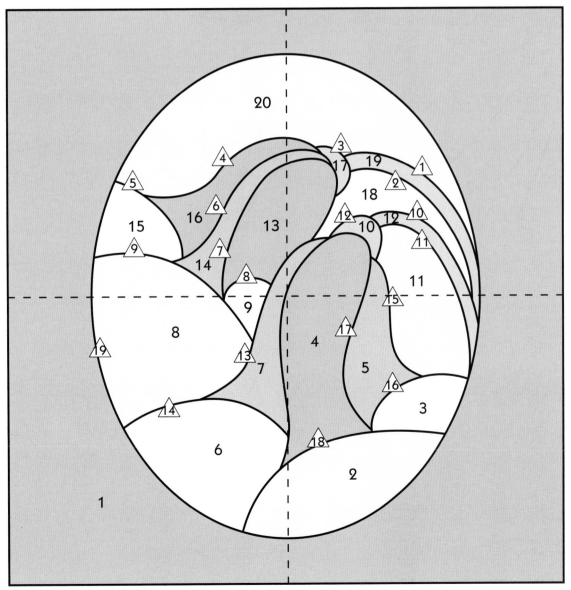

Quiet Dreams

Technique: inset Piec-liqué, page 14
layered Piec-liqué, page 18

Block size: 6" finished

Block Resizing

6"	100%
8"	134%
10"	167%
12"	200%
14"	233%
16"	267%

Quilt shown on page 104.

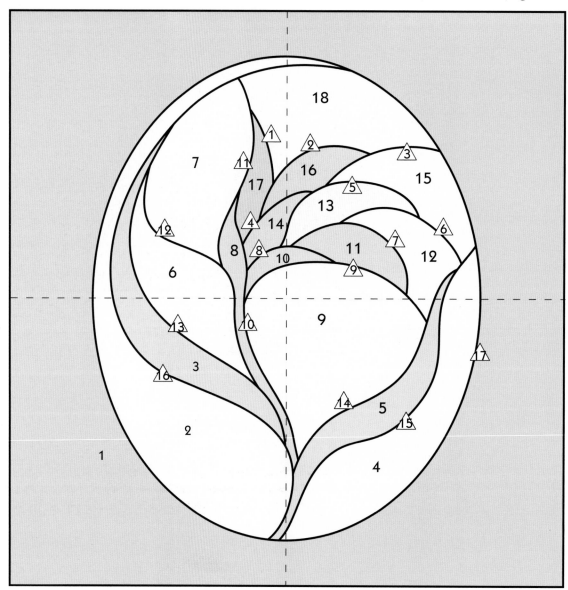

Wild Rose

Technique: inset Piec-liqué, page 14

layered Piec-liqué, page 18

Block size: 6" finished

Block Resizing

6"	100%
8"	134%
10"	167%
12"	200%
14"	233%
16"	267%

Quilt shown on page 104.

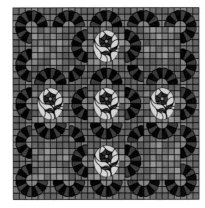

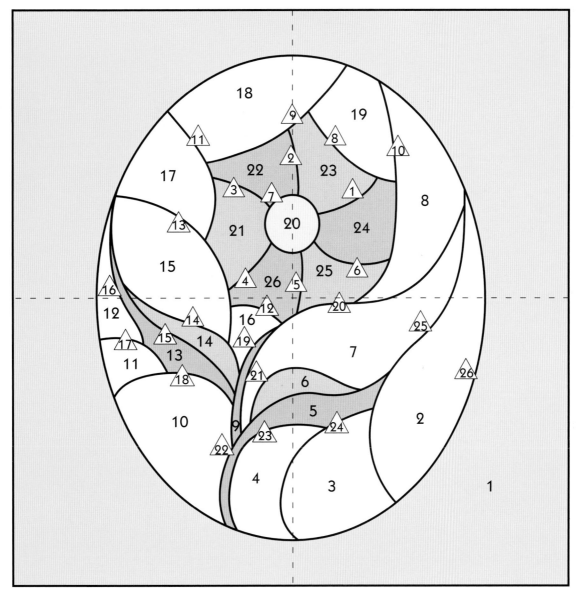

Dove of Peace

Technique: inset Piec-liqué, page 14
layered Piec-liqué, page 18

Block size: 6" finished

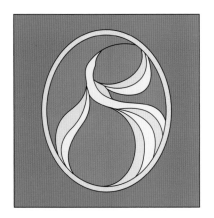

Block Resizing	
6"	100%
8"	134%
10"	167%
12"	200%
14"	233%
16"	267%

Quilt shown on page 110.

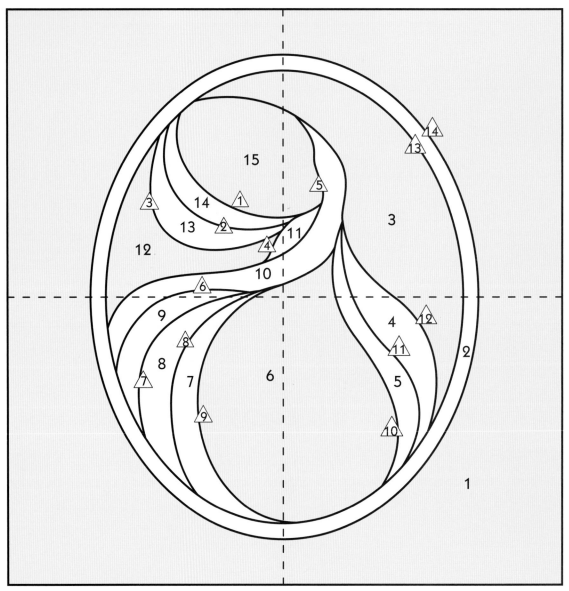

Morning Breeze

Technique: inset Piec-liqué, page 14

layered Piec-liqué, page 18

Block size: 6" finished

Block Resizing

6"	100%
8"	134%
10"	167%
12"	200%
14"	233%
16"	267%

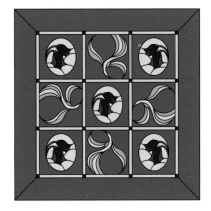

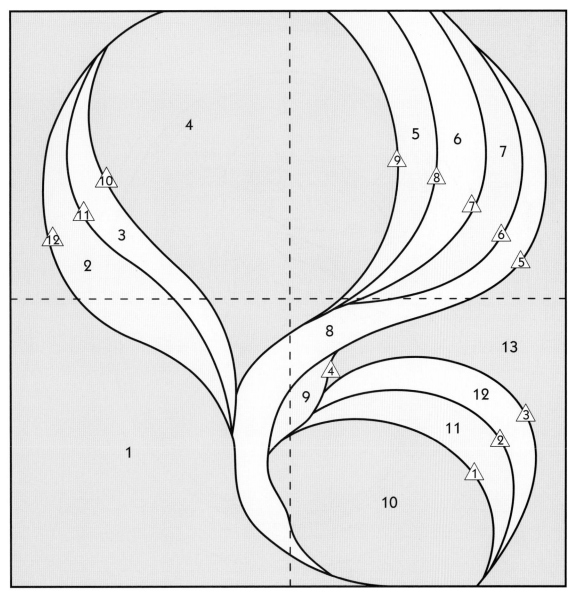

Crimson Iris

Technique: inset Piec-liqué, page 14
layered Piec-liqué, page 18

Block size: 6" finished

Block Resizing

6"	100%
8"	134%
10"	167%
12"	200%
14"	233%
16"	267%

Quilt shown on page 104.

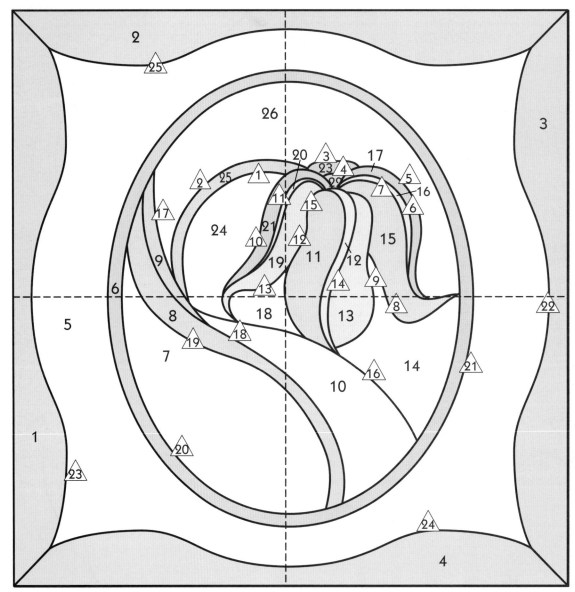

Gallery
of
Piec-liqué Quilts

SHE LED THE WAY (90" x 71"). Made by the author.

BLACK-EYED SUSAN (52" x 52"). Block pattern on page 88.

Susie Q (23½" x 40"). Block pattern on page 89.

WILD ROSE. Block pattern on page 97.

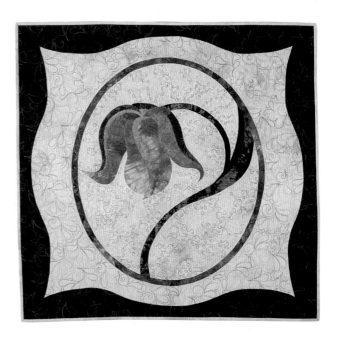

CRIMSON IRIS. Block pattern on page 100.

BLUE BELLS IN MY GARDEN. Block pattern on page 95.

QUIET DREAMS. Block pattern on page 96.

Untitled (41½" x 41½"). Made by the author.

LEANN'S PINWHEEL (86" x 86"). Block pattern on page 50.

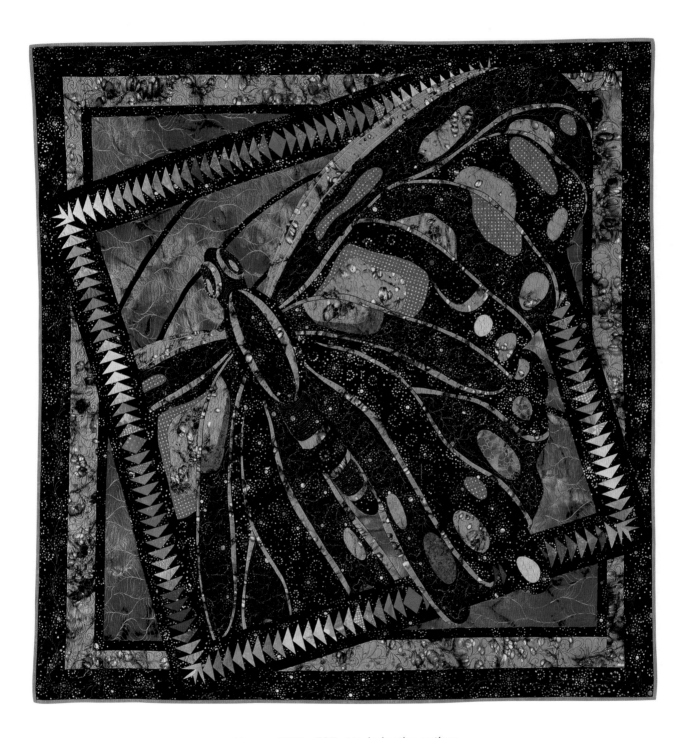

UNTITLED (50" x 50"). Made by the author.

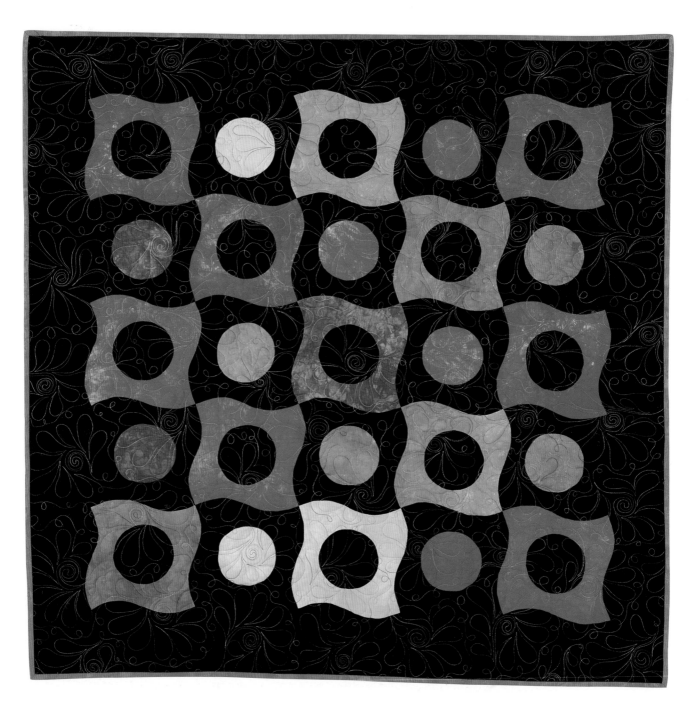

GUMBALL QUILT (36½" x 36½"). Block pattern on page 68.

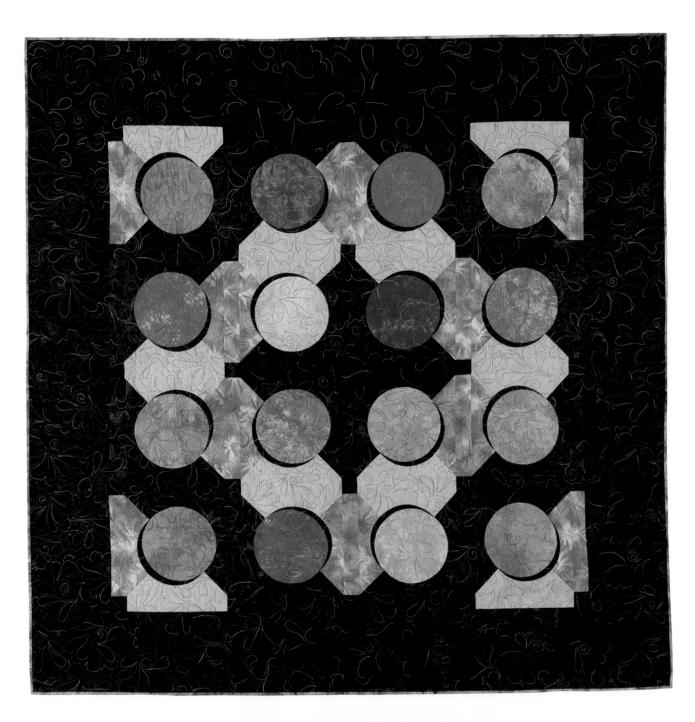

Untitled (62" x 62"). Made by the author.

DOVE OF PEACE (30½" x 30½"). Block pattern on page 98.

Meet the Author

I started my quilting just like most of you do, buying the wrong fabric, using the wrong batting, and using the wrong needles. With time, I learned to use what really works for me, even though the product might not be known as the "right" one. I do not under any circumstances compromise my standards, however.

I had to learn what a scant quarter and a fat quarter were. Translating all those unusual terms that we use so casually was the next step. The first year was just a spin of learning and creating a base for future quilts. The learning curve for a novice is quite steep. I remember my grandmother quilting, back in the '60s, but everything was so different when compared to today. I hope that the quilt world will be just as different for my grandchildren.

Living way out in the middle of nowhere as I do, there were no classes to take. I was desperate to learn what quilting was all about. I bought as many books as were available and joined my local quilt guild.

I had no idea that quilts were being machine quilted. I remember only that quilts were all hand pieced and hand quilted. I remember my Grandma Larsen counting the stitches per inch and ranting about being inconsistent, so that is where I went.

I set out to find how many stitches per inch I needed to make my quilts "right." I asked the wrong person, and she told me that it was just rude to ask. This was the first indication that I needed to be a teacher. I know that it is never rude to ask anything, if you are trying to learn a new skill.

I then started working with needle-turn appliqué. I have inherited a tremor from both of my parents, so needle-turn was out of the question. I love appliqué so much that I had to figure out another method so I could do hand appliqué and have it look like needle-turn, hence the development of Piec-liqué.

So you don't have to trace your designs, full-sized patterns are available on the author's Web site SharonSchamber.com. There are also instructional videos available to show you the techniques.

Other AQS Books

This is only a small selection of the books available from the American Quilter's Society. AQS books are known worldwide for timely topics, clear writing, beautiful color photos, and accurate illustrations and patterns. The following books are available from your local bookseller, quilt shop, or public library.

#6802   us$21.95

#6671   us$21.95

#5855   us$22.95

#6511   us$22.95

#6070   us$24.95

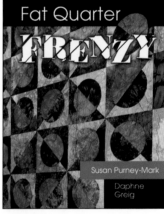

#6673   us$21.95

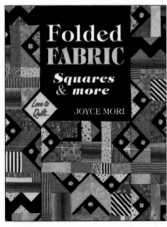

#6207   us$16.95

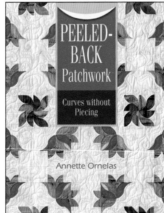

#6516   us$21.95

#6299   us$24.95

Look for these books nationally.
Call or **Visit** our Web site at

1-800-626-5420
www.AmericanQuilter.com